Prayers in the Dark

*Meditations on Suffering
from the Book of Lamentations*

LAWRENCE R. FARLEY

ANCIENT FAITH PUBLISHING
CHESTERTON, INDIANA

Published by:
Ancient Faith Publishing
A Division of Ancient Faith Ministries
1050 Broadway, Suite 6
Chesterton, IN 46304

Cover art and design by Micah Peek

ISBN: 978-1-955890-98-4

Library of Congress Control Number: 2025949024

Also by Lawrence R. Farley
for Ancient Faith Publishing

Living Faith
The Orthodox Bible Study Companion Series
(13 volumes)
The Christian Old Testament
A Song in the Furnace
A Daily Calendar of Saints
Unquenchable Fire
Following Egeria
One Flesh
The Empty Throne
Let Us Attend
The Christian Old Testament

For
the courageous
Michael and Katrina,
Amy and Trevor.
Proverbs 20:6

CONTENTS

FOREWORD

IN OUR MODERN WORLD, THERE are "experts" in every field imaginable competing for recognition and fame amid a cacophony of voices. Some become what we now call "influencers." The religious arena is no exception to this phenomenon. Created by social media, the multitude of contributors operate with little or no accountability.

So, where do we find a time-tested and reliable author who writes an exegesis of Holy Scripture that is not personal opinion? We must look for a pastor or scholar to interpret the Bible in a style that is clearly within the received Tradition of the Church. For at least four decades, the many books, articles, podcasts, blogs, and retreats associated with Archpriest Lawrence Farley have been received by faithful Christians as reliable guides.

This is true with both his Old Testament commentaries and those on the New Testament. Father Lawrence's familiarity with sacred Scripture speaks of his personal love for the Word of God. His scholarship is unquestioned. More important, I believe, is the influence of his many years of pastoral care for those entrusted to his priestly vocation. His work in biblical commentary has not been done in academic isolation but rather from the fields that are ripe for harvest. This may be his strongest qualifier as the author of the book you now hold in your hands. He has been there with his people in their sufferings and sorrows. He knows them as only a true shepherd can.

The Book of Jeremiah is the largest single corpus found in the Old Testament canon. In this commentary on the Lamentations of Jeremiah, Fr. Lawrence takes on the history of the prophet who suffered before an unfaithful Israel. Jeremiah's call to repentance becomes a call to each of us in our day. The Church is the New Israel, and we too must hear the words from Lamentations 4:20 (NKJV):

The breath of our nostrils, the anointed of
  the LORD,
Was caught in their pits,
Of whom we said, "Under his shadow
We shall live among the nations."

In the pages of *Prayers in the Dark*, the words
ascribed to Jeremiah are heard once again, and
the words of a priest become a salve for those who
suffer. Father Lawrence counts himself among the
suffering, and this is why he knows the path that
leads to salvation.

—Archpriest Chad Hatfield
President of St. Vladimir's Seminary, Retired

To Love Is to Suffer

IN WHAT IS INTENDED TO be a serious book on suffering, I would like to open, perhaps counterintuitively, with a quote from Woody Allen's movie *Love and Death*, his affectionate parody of such Russian novels as *War and Peace*. In one of the speeches given by the widow Sonja (played by the late Diane Keaton) to another widow, Natasha, she philosophizes thus:

> Natasha, to love is to suffer. To avoid suffering, one must not love. But then one suffers from not loving. Therefore, to love is to suffer. Not to love is to suffer. To suffer is to suffer. To be happy is to love. To be happy, then, is to suffer, but suffering makes one unhappy.

Therefore, to be unhappy one must love, or love to suffer, or suffer from too much happiness.... I hope you're getting this down.[1]

It's all farce, of course, in the spirit of the over-the-top parody that characterized most of Allen's early films. But beneath the farcical exterior, Allen does touch on one of the universal themes of human existence: the inevitability of suffering.

And he was not wrong: To love (that is, to be human) is to suffer, and since the capacity for giving and receiving love is basic to human nature, suffering will always be a part of life.

Moreover, even apart from love, living has always involved suffering. In support of this, I offer three simple observations that were true throughout all history until comparatively recently, each of which tells its own story:

1. Childbirth has always been dangerous; women often died in childbirth. This was why men often married more than once.

---

1   *Love and Death*, directed by Woody Allen (MGM, 1975).

2. Infant and child mortality rates were always high. In a family with ten children, it was not unusual for only half of them to reach adulthood or old age.

3. Modern anesthesia was first publicly demonstrated on October 16, 1846, which means that throughout most of human history, patients were awake during all medical treatments—including amputation.

Letting these historical facts sink in can tell us much about the prevalence and intensity of human suffering. It is an intrinsic part of human existence—and perhaps not just a part of *human* existence but of *all* sentient existence, since animals suffer as well. Nature is famously "red in tooth and claw,"[2] as the poet Alfred, Lord Tennyson wrote; animals further up the food chain kill and consume those further down the chain. Make of it what you will, death and suffering seem to be built into sentient existence.

---

2   Alfred, Lord Tennyson, "In Memorium A. H. H.," Canto 56, in *Selected Poems* (Penguin Classics, 2008), 96.

But, as we will see later, suffering in human beings is of a different order than suffering in the animal world. We experience different kinds of suffering than do our animal friends. We worry, we anguish, we grieve. Some people even contemplate and commit suicide—something animals never do. We rarely regard each day's trouble as sufficient to the day (see Matt. 6:34) but insist on importing possible future troubles into the present.

And we worry about practically everything. Will we get cancer? Die in a car or plane accident, have a stroke, or be maimed? Will we be able to pay our bills? Will we be happily married? Will our children suffer? Will *their* marriages be happy? Will *they* die prematurely? Will there be war, or economic collapse, or the imposition of tyranny? Will we suffer chronic pain before the end? When will we suffer bereavement or death? Will death be painful?

These questions are asked by all people everywhere but not by animals. Such anguish, fear, and apprehension are uniquely human characteristics and preoccupations. That is perhaps why our fears find expression and answer in the Bible. Two entire books in it are devoted to human suffering: the Book of Job and the Lamentations of Jeremiah, also known as the Book of Lamentations.

The Book of Job deals with suffering only tangentially. Despite what is often said, it is *not* an attempt to answer the question, "Why do the righteous suffer?" If that were the intention, it did not give much of an answer. Rather, the Book of Job deals with the question, "Why should the righteous be righteous?" That is, why should we be pious and worship God? The usual answer of its day was: If you are pious, God will bless you. The Book of Job replies, "Yes, but what if He *doesn't* bless you? What if you are pious and you suffer? Should you still piously worship Him?"

The Book of Job offers the lesson—revolutionary in its day—that we should worship God simply because He is God, regardless of what we "get out of it." We are not fit judges of God's justice and cosmic administration. We can't even figure out the physical world around us, much less the hidden ways of God. We worship God because He is worthy.

In contrast, the Book of the Lamentations of Jeremiah focuses more acutely upon suffering—in this case, the suffering that befell God's people in 586 BC when the Babylonians invaded the land, slaughtered the populace, and brought about its national extinction. The book delves into suffering in lurid detail, thereby exposing the contours of the human heart. Like the rest of the Scriptures, it does not offer pat answers or neat solutions, for human existence is too rich, deep, complex, varied, and mysterious for that. But by setting aside our current concerns for a while and entering the world of God's people in the sixth century BC, we can gain insights that help with our suffering. At the very least, we find assurance that we are not unique in our suffering and that the way home to the Kingdom brings pain as well as joy. As the conclusion will suggest, when we look at the life of the Master, suffering and glory coalesce as one before the suffering finally fades, leaving only the glory: It was His time on the Cross that Christ referred to as His being glorified, as His "hour."

I invite you to join me in this journey through suffering. Let us for a while leave our own tormented time and enter the world of Jerusalem and Judah when the smoke of their destruction still hung in the air. Let us find ourselves among blood-soaked ruins on a hot July day in 586 BC in what was arguably the nadir of Judah's existence as the chosen people of God. These five poems of the Lamentations of Jeremiah offer us an alphabet of suffering that can perhaps help us make sense of and cope with our own miseries.

Dateline Jerusalem, July 24, 586 BC

I T SEEMED LIKE THE END of the world. It was certainly the end of *their* world. After a horrific siege by the ruthless Babylonians, Jerusalem fell to the invaders, and most of the population that survived were carried away into exile.

To fully understand that terrible day, we need to go back not only decades but centuries. It's not as if it should have come as a surprise—after all, when Israel, newly liberated from Egypt, stood at the foot of Mount Sinai, Yahweh, the God of their fathers, entered into a covenant with them. In a word, He promised that He would be their national God and they would be His people.

What that meant was spelled out in the form of what scholars call a *suzerainty treaty*, a treaty covenant that a powerful king made with a lesser king. It specified things like why the treaty was being made (i.e., how wonderful and gracious the big king was), what the basic stipulations of the treaty were (usually things like tribute and military support), the lawyer-like details of the basic stipulations, and then what would happen afterward. That is, if the lesser king kept the treaty, certain blessings could be expected; if they violated the treaty, certain curses and retaliation could be expected. The respective gods of the nations were then invoked, and the treaty was written down and kept in a sacred place for later consultation if needed.

That in a nutshell is the form of the Book of Deuteronomy, which recapitulates the Sinai covenant—minus, of course, the invocation of the gods, since the covenant was being made by Yahweh, the only real God. In place of the invocation of the gods, Yahweh calls heaven and earth as witnesses to the covenant (see Deut. 30:19).

Note some of the curses to be invoked against Israel should they violate the covenant: not only pestilence, drought, and famine but also invasion by a foreign enemy and exile. Thus, Deuteronomy 28:49–65, which reads in part:

The LORD will bring a nation against you from afar, from the end of the earth, as swift as the eagle flies, a nation whose language you do not understand, a nation of stern countenance, who shall not regard the person of the old or show favor to the young. . . . They shall besiege you in all your towns, until your high and fortified walls, in which you trusted, come down throughout all your land . . . And you shall eat the offspring of your own body, the flesh of your sons and daughters, whom the LORD your God has given you, in the siege and in the distress with which your enemies shall distress you. . . . And the LORD will scatter you among all peoples, from one end of the earth to the other; and there you shall serve other gods, of wood and stone, which neither you nor your fathers have known. And among these nations you shall find no ease, and there shall be no rest for the sole of your foot; but the LORD will give you there a trembling heart, and failing eyes, and a languishing soul.

There's much more in the text, but you get the idea. All the prophets predicted and threatened Israel and Judah with this very doom if they did not repent and turn back to Yahweh. But Israel and Judah *did* break Yahweh's covenant, year after year and century after century, worshipping other deities, serving idols, refusing to walk in justice, grinding the faces of the poor. All the prophets urged repentance, and all their prophetic warnings were ignored. At length, in 586 BC, the final judgment fell.

Prelude to Judgment

WE CAN LOOK AT THE immediate background to this judgment by reading the Book of Jeremiah.

There was even a foretaste of the final judgment in 597 BC when the foreign foe invaded and carried into exile the king and certain other nobles. (Read all about it in 2 Kings 24.) A puppet king, Zedekiah, was installed, who was but twenty-one years old at the time.

You would've thought that after the invasion in 597 BC the people of Jerusalem and Judah would have gotten the message and repented. Nope—not at all. The nationalistic prophets (*false* prophets, as it turned out) predicted that the exile of the king and his nobles was but a temporary setback—that they would soon return, and all would be well. Let Judah carry on courageously and stay the (idolatrous) course! Sadly, the people did, with the inevitable result.

The Babylonian victory in 597 BC was not ultimately rooted in Babylonian military might but in Yahweh's plan to judge His people. Therefore, as we read:

And in the ninth year of [Zedekiah's] reign, in the tenth month, on the tenth day of the month [i.e., March 25], Nebuchadnez'zar king of Babylon came with all his army against Jerusalem, and laid siege to it; and they built siegeworks against it round about. So the city was besieged till the eleventh year of King Zedeki'ah. On the ninth day of the fourth month [i.e., July 24] the famine was so severe in the city that there was no food for the people of the land. Then a breach was made in the city; the king with all the men of war fled by night by the way of the gate between the two walls, by the king's garden, though the Chalde'ans were around the city. And they went in the direction of the Arabah. But the army of the Chalde'ans pursued the king and overtook him in the plains of Jericho; and all his army was scattered from him. Then they captured the king, and brought him up to the king of Babylon at Riblah, who passed sentence upon him. They slew the sons of Zedeki'ah before his eyes, and put out the eyes of Zedeki'ah, and bound him in fetters, and took him to Babylon. (2 Kings 25:1–7)

The conciseness of the biblical narrative scarcely does justice to the horror, the terror, and the despair of the people who were then starving to the point of cannibalism within the city. The loss of their king and of their temple—the one place in the world where they could find access to their God by sacrifice—meant national extinction. Israel in the north had ceased to exist after the Assyrians crushed it in 732 bc, and now it was Judah's turn. They also would cease to exist as a nation, doomed to be swallowed up and assimilated by the hated Babylonian superpower.

Furthermore, they had been betrayed by their neighbors, racial kin such as the Edomites from whom they might have expected aid or at least sympathy. But no: They were abandoned, mocked, and derided by all. Everyone around them exulted over Judah's fall and their misery, delighting in their every howl of pain, their every wound.

We see some of this raw pain in Psalm 137:7–9, which reads:

> Remember, O Lord, against the E'domites
> the day of Jerusalem,

how they said, "Raze it, raze it!
   Down to its foundations!"
O daughter of Babylon, you devastator!
   Happy shall he be who requites you
   with what you have done to us!
Happy shall he be who takes your
   little ones
   and dashes them against the rock!

This is not the voice of vindictiveness. It is the voice of despair, the voice of young men who stood by and watched while their wives and daughters were raped over and over again, whose pregnant women had their bellies cut open, who watched while their fathers and grandfathers were butchered before their eyes—men who watched while laughing invaders took their infants by their ankles and dashed their brains out against the rocks. The psalmist is here crying out to God, "How could You let this happen to us?"

Poetry of Grief and Suffering

AFTER ALL THIS, WHAT REMAINED for Jerusalem and Judah? The answer can be found in the

Lamentations of Jeremiah. The short Book of Lamentations, usually treated as a mere footnote to the Book of Jeremiah and often skipped over, is a collection of five acrostic poems, with each stanza beginning with a letter of the Hebrew alphabet.[3] They represent the authentic voice of exilic Israel—a mourner's wailing over what had befallen them and an attempt to make sense of it all. Reading it over, one can almost see the tears that fell upon the original pages and smell the smoke of the burning city, which lingered long in the air. The whole of the little book is soaked in trauma and blood.

Such grief may therefore help us with insight as we experience our own griefs. Comparisons, of course, are impossible. How can one compare the suffering of Jerusalem with the suffering of a parent who has watched their child sicken and die of cancer at a young age? Or the suffering of someone struggling with clinical depression, for whom every dawning day is a new disaster, another temptation to suicide? Or the suffering of a single

---

3   The fifth poem, a prayer for restoration, is not acrostic in form.

parent who cannot put enough food on the table, whose children must go to bed each night hungry and crying? Or the suffering of those forced to live under regimes of tyranny and persecution? Only God can measure, compare, and calibrate such misery.

Here I can only offer biblical exegesis and pastoral meditation. In what follows, I will paraphrase the sacred text and exegete the passage according to its original meaning. After each poem, I will then offer a meditation on human suffering—not to explain or ameliorate it (this is well beyond any human ability) but to point a way forward into hope. Each meditation uses a line of the preceding poem as a jumping-off point. In other words, the meditations are not intended as further commentary on or exegesis of the poems but as musings on the various kinds of suffering to which humanity is subjected.

Christians know that our hope has a name: Jesus of Nazareth, the hope of the hopeless, the Savior of the bestormed, the haven of the voyager, the physician of the sick, the One who knows each person and their individual request, each home and each need. All our hope is in Christ. He is the One who suffered as we suffer, taking upon Himself the sins and sufferings of the world. He is the man of pains, acquainted with sickness (Is. 53:3, literal Hebrew). He is the One who knew loneliness and poverty, having nowhere to lay His head. He is the One who wept at the grave of Lazarus, His friend. He is the One who was betrayed by His close companion, the one who ate bread from His plate. He lived in a land occupied by a hated and invincible foreign power, with no hope of liberation. He was God's suffering servant. And He is the One who never abandons us in our own suffering, but who catches our tears and treasures them (Ps. 56:8). All our hope is in Him.

A Few Notes for Scholarly Types

IN THE MASORETIC HEBREW, THE Lamentations of Jeremiah is an anonymous book and nowhere ascribed to the prophet Jeremiah. That ascription comes from the Septuagint, which appends the work to the Books of Jeremiah and Baruch and begins by saying, "And this happened after Israel was taken captive and Jerusalem was devastated: Jeremiah sat down weeping, and he wailed this lament over Jerusalem and said . . ." Then follows what is verse 1 in the Masoretic, "How alone lies the city packed with people." In the Masoretic Bible, the Book of Lamentations is not attached to the Books of Jeremiah and Baruch among the Prophets but is found later among the Writings.

In the Masoretic Bible, the Book of Lamentations is called the "Book of How," taking its name, as did other ancient books, from the book's first word, "how." The word occurs at the beginning of poem one and is repeated at the beginning of poems two and four. The English word *how* is the Hebrew *'ekah*, a word that sounds like a gasp, appropriate for what follows it. *'Ekah* is more like the cry of "alas!" than a simple interrogative. The Septuagint entitles the book *Threnoi*, meaning "brooding laments."

The five poems in the book have no obvious relation to one another, and there is no obvious development between one poem and the next. There is also no reason to think that the prophet Jeremiah actually wrote any of the poems, the Septuagint's guess notwithstanding. Authorship in the ancient world would ascribe a work to a well-known figure regardless of the actual author. The prophet Jeremiah (often referred to as "the weeping prophet," from his words in Jeremiah 14:17) was an obvious literary choice, as the poems were written in such a spirit of weeping lamentation.

There is also no reason to conclude that the same person wrote all five poems, though they might have. The fact that the fifth poem, unlike the first four poems, is not acrostic suggests that the book represents a collection of works by different authors, for an author committed to acrostic poetry would probably have written all five poems in that form.

The acrostic or alphabetical nature of the poems also calls for further comment. Like some of the acrostic psalms (such as Psalm 119, which is the longest and most memorable), this may serve a mnemonic purpose. But perhaps the alphabetical structure was also chosen to express the totality of suffering, a kind of "misery from A to Z" (or from *aleph* to *taw*): The poems include every kind of suffering, just as the alphabet includes every single letter.

The voices of the speaker vary in the poems. Some chapters present the voice of a woman, the daughter of Zion herself, bewailing her own fall and misery (e.g., 1:11f). Some sections present the voice of a third-person narrator lamenting the suffering of the daughter of Zion. Another poem presents the voice of a man, an eyewitness and participant in the trauma (3:1f). The total effect (doubtless intended) is to offer an interplay of voices, representing the variegated misery of everyone in the city.

The Book of Lamentations, therefore, is a book of pain and grief and perplexity, a brutal book, a book that desperately seeks an audience with God but finds Him hidden and inaccessible, a God who hides Himself in a time of calamity. It is a hard book for us to read in our culture of affluence, ease, health, pleasure, and entitlement. But perhaps that is just why we need such a book, more than ever. Much of the world does not enjoy the affluence, health, pleasure, and entitlement that characterize the West and, though too often hidden from view, many in the West do not enjoy such things in unbroken serenity either. The Book of Lamentations is a book of suffering—a book for a suffering humanity.

A Note on Translation

THE PARAPHRASE OF THE LAMENTATIONS of Jeremiah that follows is mine. I have divided the scriptural text of each poem into sections, with commentary following each section. Citations from the biblical text are present in the commentary in **boldface**.

Lamentations Poem One

1:1–11a   *No Comfort for Zion!*

> ¹ Ah, how alone sits the city
>   once packed with people!
> She is now a widow,
>   though once great among the nations!
> The princess among the provinces
>   has become a vassal.
> ² She weeps bitterly in the night,
>   tears on her cheeks;
> among all her lovers
>   she finds no comforter;
> all her friends have betrayed her
>   and become her enemies.

As noted in the Historical Introduction, the text opens with the Hebrew *'ekah*, a word like a gasp, a catch in the throat, here rendered "**Ah, how.**"

There is a note of shock, of surprise. The narrator is stunned by the contrast: Earlier, the city was thronging with people, bustling with merchants and buyers, old men and children, **packed with people**, everyone getting on with their busy lives. Now it is a ghost town, **sitting** lonely and **alone** on a hill. (Sitting was the posture of mourning in that culture.) **Though once great among the nations**, a city respected for its power and influence, **she is now a widow**. Widows in the ancient world were not just alone but bereaved of all protection, utterly vulnerable to any who would take advantage of them, and completely without hope. Jerusalem had gone from power to poverty, from strength to vulnerability, all at one stroke.

The contrast continues. Once Jerusalem was a **princess among the** outer **provinces** (those places once controlled by Judah), a noblewoman commanding respect, with money at hand to fulfill her every desire. Now she is **a vassal**, utterly beholden to the powerful she once commanded, reduced to paying them tribute. No wonder she **weeps bitterly in the night** when none can see her tears and all others sleep soundly: **Among all her**

lovers and protectors, she **finds no comforter**, no one to help pay her bills, to bring her relief. The term *lovers* hints at immoral relationships—"sugar daddies"—since respectable women of that time had husbands or fathers to protect them, not lovers (see, for example, Ezek. 16:15f).

Worse yet, **all her friends have betrayed her and become her enemies**. Nowadays we use the term *friend* far too easily, as users of Facebook will attest. In the ancient world, a friend was an ally, someone who had your back at all times, someone you could count on when things got tough. How terrible to find that these allies had now abandoned her and gone over to the side of her enemies.

These verses personify the city of Jerusalem as a woman; many cities in the ancient Near East were personified as women, as the wives of their protecting deities. The political reality behind the poetry is that the city of Jerusalem had suffered the ultimate catastrophe, with dead bodies rotting in the streets, the population greatly reduced and impoverished, and no remaining infrastructure. None of her former allies would offer help or even sympathy; the Babylonian superpower was too strong to allow them such a risk. In modern terms, no one would return Jerusalem's phone calls. Wounded and on the verge of dying, she was on her own.

> ³ Judah is exiled after her affliction
>   and hard slavery.
> She sits among the nations now
>   but finds no resting place there;
> her pursuers have all overtaken her
>   between her straits.
> ⁴ The roads to Zion mourn,
>   for now no one comes to her festivals;
> all her gates are deserted;
>   her priests groan;
> her virgins have been stricken,
>   and she herself suffers bitterly.

The camera now pulls back from the city of Jerusalem to survey Judah as a whole, for the whole nation has witnessed the fall of its capital. **After her affliction and hard slavery**, her crushing defeat and the fastening of slavery's fetters, the whole nation of **Judah** was **exiled**. The survivors were bound together and began the long march to Babylon, where they would be slaves, never to see their homes, families, or friends again. Home was home no longer. Judah **sat** not in the Promised Land but **among the nations now**, strangers in a strange land; no longer would they hear the familiar speech of hearth and home, instead the rough, unintelligible babble of foreigners. Yet even **there** they would **find no resting place**. The reference is to Deuteronomy 28:65: "Among these nations you shall find no ease, and there shall be no rest for the sole of your foot." The covenant curse was now upon them. **Her pursuers had all overtaken her** and brought her down.

A quick look around confirmed this. Normally the festival days, such as Passover, were days of lively joy. In our culture, entertainment, religion, music, and feasting tend to be separate things, but it was otherwise in the ancient Near East. All of life was one. Festivals were not just religious events (as dreary as that can sound to us moderns) but times of family and feasting, of music and dancing and celebration. The Psalter witnesses to this unity of exuberance. Psalm 42:4 speaks of going with the throng "in procession to the house of God," a voice of joy and thanksgiving, "a multitude keeping festival"—a happy hubbub indeed!

But now, there were no such crowds thronging the roads and filling the air with joyful singing and shouting. The **roads to Zion mourned**, quiet and deserted, for **now no one** was left to **come to her festivals**. Zion's city **gates**, a place of business and busyness, were **deserted** too. Zion's **priests**, left in the city, **groan** for lack of their livelihood and support, for no one comes to Zion to offer sacrifice anymore. Zion's **virgins**, the young unmarried girls, **have been stricken**, struck down and despairing, with no hope of marriage and future. The whole city **suffers bitterly**.

> [5] Her foes have become the head;
>   her enemies prosper
> because Yahweh has struck her
>   for her many transgressions;
> her babies have left as captives,
>   driven before the foe.

⁶ From the daughter of Zion
    all her majesty has departed:
her princes have become like deer
    that find no pasture,
melting away without strength
    before their pursuer.

Judah's **foes**, formerly no threat and kept in subjection, **have** now **become the head**, with Judah the tail (another reference to the covenant curses; see Deut. 28:44). This humiliation was the result not only of the military supremacy of **her enemies** but of **Yahweh,** who **struck** Judah **for her many transgressions**. Most grievous of all these humiliations was that **her babies left as captives, driven before the foe**.

The word here rendered as *babies* is the Hebrew *'olaleha*, meaning not only sons and children but all beloved and cherished children regardless of age. It is the cry mothers make when their young children are wrenched from their arms: "My baby!" It was these beloved offspring who were taken from their mothers, tied together with ropes, and led away to be slaves, **driven before the foe** who took them captive, never to be seen by their families again.

In short, the **majesty of the daughter of Zion** had forever **departed**—a reference to her **princes** and nobles. Instead of standing to fight and defend, they fled **like deer** that dart away looking for **pasture**, only to finally **melt away without strength before their pursuer**, taken down, captured, totally useless.

> [7] Jerusalem remembers
>> in the days of her affliction and
>>> wandering
> all the precious things
>> that were hers from before.
> When her people fell into the power of
>> the enemy,
>> with none to help her,
> her enemies gloated over her;
>> they laughed at her downfall.
> [8] Jerusalem sinned grievously
>> and became unclean;
> all who honored her despise her,
>> for they have seen her nakedness

while she groans
    and turns her face away.
⁹ Her filthiness clings to her skirts;
    she never thought this would be her end;
therefore she has gone down terribly
    and has no comforter.

The narrator now goes on to detail Jerusalem's losses and humiliation, making her predicament all the more vivid. **Her** misery was made all the worse when **Jerusalem remembered** the way it had been before she was **wandering**, helpless and homeless, when she had access to **all the precious things that were hers from before**—the temple, her palaces, her wealth, her security, her freedom, her honor.

All this has utterly vanished. When **her people fell into the power of the enemy**, **her enemies gloated over her** and **laughed at her downfall**, making her powerlessness all the more galling.

The narrator then turns to diagnosis and cause: This all happened because **Jerusalem sinned grievously and became unclean**. In Western culture, we have no corresponding category for ritual uncleanness. Menstruation is no longer thought to render a woman ritually unclean, any more than touching a dead body does. In the ancient Near East, however, both rendered a person unclean and untouchable.

This metaphor of ritual uncleanness explains why Jerusalem's allies would not help or touch her. They would not touch her any more than one would touch an unclean woman. And the uncleanness was Jerusalem's fault. Though they formerly **honored** her, her allies now **despised** her and withdrew. Why? They had **seen her nakedness**, and **her filthiness** (her menstrual blood, so to speak) **clung to her skirts**, making her unclean. The metaphor of ritual uncleanness, which brought no moral stigma, merges with moral uncleanness, Jerusalem's idolatry. It was for this moral uncleanness that God left Jerusalem vulnerable to attack. She **never thought** that worshipping idols would bring her to such an **end**, so she **went down terribly**, with **no comforter** or helper.

> [9b] "Yahweh, behold my affliction,
>   for the enemy has triumphed!"

¹⁰ The oppressor has laid his hands
    on all her precious things,
for she has seen the nations
    enter her sanctuary,
those whom you forbade
    to enter your assembly.
¹¹ All her people groan
    as they search for bread;
they barter their treasures for food
    to keep alive.

The narrator's voice is now interrupted by a cry from the sufferer himself: **"Yahweh, behold my affliction, for the enemy has triumphed!"** The outrage was terrible and terrifying. The pagan **oppressor** had **laid his hands on all her precious things**, such as the gold of the temple and the sacred worship utensils that only priests may touch. The **nations** had **entered her sanctuary**, the Holy of Holies—the very nations whom God **forbade** to do so or to **enter** His worshipping **assembly** in the temple.

As for that assembly that used to stand before God in honor? Now they **groan** with hunger as

they **search for bread** in a barren countryside and
barter their treasures for food to keep alive. An
enemy triumph indeed!

1:11b–22 *"I have none to comfort me!"*

"Look, Yahweh, and see
    how despised I am!
¹²"Is it nothing to you, all you who pass by?
    See and look
if there is any sorrow like the sorrow
    that fell on me,
with which Yahweh struck me
    on the day of his fierce anger.
¹³"From on high he sent fire
    deep down into my bones;
he laid a snare for my feet;
    he brought me down
and left me unconscious,
    faint all the day long.
¹⁴"My transgressions became my yoke;
    he fastened it together
and set it on my neck;
    he made my strength fail;

the Lord gave me up
    to those whom I cannot resist.
¹⁵ "The Lord spurned
    all the bravest fighters in my midst;
he summoned an army against me
    to crush my young men.
The Lord has trampled as in a wine press
    the virgin daughter of Judah.
¹⁶ "That is why I weep
    and my eyes run with tears,
for a comforter is far from me
    who could revive my life;
my sons despair,
    for the enemy is too strong."

The daughter of Zion interrupts the narrator with a cry of pain, a plea to God: **"Look, Yahweh, and see how despised I am!"** It is not a cry for attention but for help. None of her former friends and allies will help her; her only remaining hope is in God. Will He not help her?

Her plea is met with silence; God will not answer. She therefore turns to **all who pass by,** strangers on the street. **Is it nothing to you?**

Are you completely heartless? Surely my suffering must touch your heart. **See and look if there is any sorrow like the sorrow that fell on me!** Surely my plight must wring your heart and elicit some sympathy and aid.

The daughter of Zion then details her pain: From on high, God sent down fire, a snare, and a yoke, stamping on her as one stamps on grapes in a winepress. **From on high**, from His very throne in heaven, God **sent fire** to fry her **bones**, scorching to a crisp her health and vitality. He **laid a snare for** her **feet**, tripping her up and capturing her; He **brought** her **down**, leaving her **unconscious** and too **faint** to help herself. He made a **yoke** from her **transgressions** and **fastened it** on her **neck**, keeping her bound and captive. He **gave** her up to her foes, whom she could **not resist**. God spurned and crushed Zion's army, the **bravest fighters in** the **midst** of the city, ready for action, for God **summoned an army against** them, like one calling worshippers to a feast.

Through their defeat, God **trampled** on the **virgin daughter of Judah** as thoroughly as grapes are **trampled** and crushed **in a winepress**. All these outrages were done to the daughter of Zion, a female figure. In that culture, such outrages on a female body pointed to rape, to unspeakable things that should not be done.[4] No wonder she **wept** and her **eyes ran with tears**. Any **comforter** who could offer first aid was **far** away; there was no one to **revive** her national life. Her **sons**, the survivors, could only **despair**.

> [17] Zion stretches out her hands for help,
>   but there is none to comfort her.
> Yahweh has summoned against Jacob
>   enemies all around him.
> Jerusalem has become
>   an unclean thing among them.

In the interplay of voices, the narrator then interrupts the daughter of Zion with a kind of newscaster's summation: **Zion stretches out her hands for help, but there is none to comfort her. Jacob** (a term denoting Zion as the covenant

---

4   Kathleen M. O'Conner, *The Book of Lamentations*, New Interpreter's Bible Commentary, Vol. IV (Abingdon Press, 2015), 890.

people) was surrounded and taken down. The victory of his **enemies all around him** came from **Yahweh**, who **summoned** them for this terrible work. The result: **Jerusalem has become an unclean thing among** the nations that no one will touch or help. The word here rendered "**unclean thing**" is *nidda*, the Hebrew word used to describe a menstrual rag.

> ¹⁸"Yahweh is indeed in the right,
>   for I have rebelled against his word.
> Listen up, all you peoples,
>   see my suffering!
> My girls and my young men
>   are exiled!
> ¹⁹"I called for help to my lovers,
>   but they deceived me;
> my priests and elders
>   perished inside the city
> while they looked for food
>   to keep them alive.
> ²⁰"Look, Yahweh, for I am in anguish;
>   my stomach churns;
> my heart is flipped over within me

because I was a rebel.
Outside the sword makes childless;
    inside it is like death.
²¹ "They heard my groaning,
    yet there is no one to comfort me.
All my enemies have heard of my calamity;
    they are glad that you have done it!
You have brought the day you foretold;
    let them become like me!
²² "Let all their wickedness come before
    you,
    and deal with them
as you have dealt with me
    because of all my transgressions;
many are my groans;
    my heart is weak."

The daughter of Zion again interrupts. The interplay of mutual interruption serves to emphasize Zion's pain: She cannot keep quiet about her distress. She declares that **Yahweh** was **indeed in the right** (literally "is righteous"), for she had **rebelled against His word**, violating the covenant and ignoring the prophets He had sent to warn her. Yet despite this admission, the daughter of Zion still calls out for sympathy because of her great suffering. "**Listen up, all you peoples**," she cries, "**see my suffering!**"

Again, she sets forth the gory details: **My girls** (literally young "virgins") **and my young men are exiled!** That is, the youth of the nation—its only hope for survival in the future—are now gone. During the day of disaster, the daughter of Zion **called for help to** her **lovers**, those who had pledged their undying love and loyalty, only to find that they had **deceived** her and would not come to her aid. And not only had the youth perished from the land as they left for exile, but the older generation of **priests and elders** who stayed **perished inside the city while they looked for food to keep them alive**. Wherever one looked, near or far, there was nothing but disaster and doom.

Faced with this, the daughter of Zion turns again to Yahweh, asking Him to look and see her **anguish**. Her **stomach churns, her heart is flipped over** in unceasing torment—all because she **was a rebel**. She repeats herself: There is nothing left but death—**outside the sword makes**

childless and **inside it is like death**, for starvation and pestilence stalk them and will soon overtake them.

Her plight is made worse by the indifference of those who betrayed her: They **heard** her **groaning** but ignored it. They **heard of** her **calamity**, and far from being sympathetic, they were **glad** of it!

She ends with a prayer for retribution on her betrayers: **Let them become like me! Let all their wickedness come before You, and deal with them as You have dealt with me.** That is, her only comfort now is the thought of future justice when the nations will get what they deserve too. Her **heart** is **weak** and failing; she can say no more. Yahweh does not reply.

First Meditation:
The Suffering of Betrayal

All her friends have betrayed her and become her enemies. (1:2)

BETRAYAL IS WHAT WE HUMAN beings do. It is one of the sad things that characterizes us as human. Animals do not betray, just as they do not sin. Rather, they simply act according to their natures. Animals will attack and feed on one another, and they generally recognize their enemies. When an African zebra sees a lion approaching, it doesn't wonder whether it is an enemy or merely a neighbor stretching its leonine legs. It knows the lion is an enemy, and it runs away. The zebras do not knowingly betray one another; they all run away together—some more quickly than others, to the distress of the slowest. Attacks in the animal world are honest affairs. When lions attack zebras, there is no duplicity or malice involved. That is why animals cannot sin, for attacking other animals is part of how they were meant to function.

Sadly, it is otherwise in the world of humankind, where sin abounds and in fact characterizes our species. Human beings betray one another—perhaps not often and doubtless with varying degrees of malice, but betrayal is a part of how we roll. It can be done out of spite, or for money, ego, or advancement. And when someone is lacking self-awareness, it can even be done unconsciously. But it is a common enough sin that if you live long enough, you will almost certainly be betrayed. *Et tu, Brute?*

Betrayal is, of course, worse than mere attack. Attacks are expected from enemies. When the Turks besieged Constantinople in 1453, it was expected that the Turkish armies would kill and pillage if they could. It was the betrayal of the city by one of its own that opened the city to the invaders, which hurt more. It is possible to regard the attack of an enemy in war with a certain degree of equanimity—after all, the attacking soldiers are just following orders. And even if the enemy is filled with malice—a malice that makes such equanimity impossible—his hostility is at least expected. What makes betrayal so hurtful is that it is always unexpected. The one you regarded as a friend, ally, and comrade suddenly turns against you and strikes. This attack is invincible because it was unanticipated.

We see this in stories ancient and modern. In the Psalter, we see an example of how unbearable and wounding is the attack of one previously regarded as a friend:

> It is not an enemy who taunts me—
>   then I could bear it;
> it is not an adversary who deals
>   insolently with me—
>   then I could hide from him.
> But it is you, my equal,
>   my companion, my familiar friend.
> We used to hold sweet converse together;
>   within God's house we walked in
>   fellowship. (Ps. 55:12–14)

We see this also in a modern story from the *Firefly* television series. In one episode, the captain of the ship, Mal, turns on someone who betrayed one of his crew—and therefore betrayed them all—by savagely saying, "The next time you decide to stab me in the back, have the guts to do it to my face!" In all stories, ancient and modern, it is the surprise of the betrayal that wounds and makes the traitor so much more terrible than a known enemy.

Those whose betrayals are well-known leave their names for a curse. Consider Vidkun Quisling or Benedict Arnold. And, of course, Judas Iscariot, whose betrayal so defined him that when St. John mentioned another Judas in his Gospel, he took care to describe him as "Judas (not Iscariot)" (John 14:22). Calling anyone a Quisling, a Benedict Arnold, or a Judas constitutes a terrible accusation.

Because the human capacity for betrayal is so universal, perhaps it was inevitable that our Lord should meet His end through such an act. Humanly speaking, betrayal was not necessary—He could have been arrested in public with honest and open force. As we learn from Mark 14:1–2, a public arrest was strategically risky but still not impossible. And given that the inner circle of disciples consisted not of five hundred or one hundred or even several dozens but of only twelve, it might have seemed unlikely that a traitor could be found among them. But so it was.

I suggest that given our human condition, with our tragic capacity for misunderstanding, backroom scheming, bribery, political cowardice, envy, hostility, bullying, brutality, lying, and betrayal, it was fitting and inevitable that all these came into play at the end of our Lord's life. He not only took upon Himself the sins of the world but recapitulated in His life all the experiences of suffering people in every generation. We find ourselves victims of scheming, bribery, and brutality, so the Master of all endured these Himself.

Tender and naïve souls might imagine that such betrayal would be foreign to our life in the Church. After all, did not the Master command us to love one another as He loved us? Alas, even superficial experience in church life reveals that this is not so. Apparently, no one in the Church is immune to such temptation—not bishops, priests, deacons, or laypersons. History reminds us that St. John Chrysostom was persecuted and betrayed by another bishop, Archbishop Theophilus of Alexandria.

One perhaps should not be surprised by all this, since in Christ's Parable of the Good Samaritan the two who first saw the injured man lying on the road and "passed by on the other side" were clergy—a priest and a Levite (Luke 10:31–32). If such things can happen in the Church, where we always have Christ before our eyes as an example of self-sacrificial love, they can happen anywhere. We should therefore never be surprised that betrayal sometimes forms a part of the fabric of our existence.

What is the lesson for us? To be true to God and to keep bitterness far from our hearts, because we are not somehow immune to the temptation to betray. Let us be unflinchingly honest with ourselves: Whether or not we betray our family, friends, or neighbors, all of us betray our God. We repay His constant and abundant love with ingratitude, sin, and hardness of heart. The opposite of love is not hatred but apathy. Humanity breaks the heart of God by ignoring Him, by living most often as if He does not exist and has no significance in our daily lives. What is that but the ultimate betrayal?

And so, God allows us to be betrayed in turn. Perhaps the pain of betrayal can turn to blessing— if it brings self-awareness of how we live and how we *should* live. Judas betrayed Christ but did not allow his regret to become actual repentance. Peter betrayed Him and went out and wept bitterly, and so he remained to experience forgiveness and restoration. Let us not give Christ a kiss as did Judas. Let us follow Peter and seek to betray Him no more. And let us return acts of betrayal with acts of love, turning the other cheek. It is what the Master did and what He commands us to do also.

Lamentations Poem Two

2:1–10   *Yahweh's Rage Against His People*

¹ Ah, how the Lord in his anger
  has brought darkness to the daughter
    of Zion!
He has cast down from heaven to earth
  the beauty of Israel,
no longer remembering his footstool
  in the day of his anger.
² The Lord has mercilessly swallowed up
  all the homes of Jacob;
in his wrath he has smashed
  the strongholds of the daughter of
    Judah;
he has thrown them to the ground,
  profaning
    the kingdom and its rulers.

³ He has cut down in burning anger
    all the power of Israel;
he has withdrawn from them his strength
    as the enemy approached;
he has burned in Jacob like a raging fire,
    consuming everything.
⁴ He has bent his bow like an enemy,
    steadying his hand like a foe,
and he has killed all that was pleasant to
    the sight;
    in the tent of the daughter of Zion
he has poured out his rage like fire.
⁵ The Lord has been like an enemy;
    he has swallowed up Israel;
he has swallowed up all its palaces;
    he has brought down in ruins its
        strongholds,
and he has multiplied in the daughter
    of Judah,
    mourning and weeping.
⁶ He has wrecked his tent like a garden,
    brought down in ruins his place of
        meeting.
Yahweh wiped out the very memory

of festival and Sabbath,
and in his fiery rage has rejected king
 and priest.
⁷ The Lord has despised his altar,
 hated his sanctuary;
he has delivered into the enemy's power
 her palace walls;
they made an uproar in the house of
  Yahweh
 as on the day of festival.
⁸ Yahweh decided to bring down in ruins
 the wall of the daughter of Zion;
he measured it up
 and did not stop until it was destroyed,
bringing lamentation to the ramparts and
 walls—
 they lay dejected together!
⁹ Her gates have sunk to the ground;
 he has broken and shattered her bars.
Her king and princes are among the
 nations;
 the Law is no more,
and her prophets find
 no vision from Yahweh.

¹⁰ The elders of the daughter of Zion
    sit on the ground reduced to silence;
they have sprinkled dust on their heads
    and put on sackcloth;
the girls of Jerusalem
    hang their heads down to the ground.

The **darkness** that the Lord **brought** to **the daughter of Zion** was that of ruin and total destruction. In Hebrew the word used is *'uwb*, meaning "beclouded," so that versions such as the King James render it "covered with a cloud." To us this might suggest merely a cloudy day, whereas it originally meant the coming of darkness (hence the New English Bible's "What darkness the Lord has brought"). The cloud was a black thundercloud, for after the catastrophe of 586 BC, the horizon was not a little cloudy but dark—a night with no light of hope in sight.

The **beauty of Israel**, God's holy temple, seemed to reach up to God's throne in heaven. Indeed, the temple *was* the earthly throne of the heavenly God. Yet **in the day of His anger** toward His people, God **cast** it **down from heaven to earth**, severing His link with them, **no longer remem-bering** or caring about **His** earthly **footstool**.

And not just *His* earthly home, but *theirs*! He **mercilessly swallowed up all the homes of Jacob**, God's covenant people, as the invaders burned them to the ground along with all **Judah's strongholds**. The **kingdom** (the royal family and the royal line) and Judah's **rulers** God **profaned**, treating them as worthless, no longer sacred, and refusing to defend them. **All the power of Israel** (literally "the horn of Israel"), its valiant soldiers, He **cut down in His burning anger**. As **the enemy approached** them, He **withdrew from them His strength**, leaving them helpless and doomed. The result was a total holocaust, with everything **burned** up and sacrificed, the **raging fire** of God's wrath **consuming everything** in sight. It was as if God were an enemy soldier, **bending His bow**, **steadying** it, and carefully taking aim at His people. God thus **killed all that was** once **pleasant** in His **sight**—all their fine young men rushing to defend His **tent**, His holy temple. Temple, **palaces**, **strongholds**—all came crashing down, and in their place, He left nothing but **mourning and**

weeping. Wherever one went, there was nothing but the sound of heartbreak.

It was the destruction of the temple that was hardest to bear. God **wrecked** His **tent** (the temple) as easily and thoughtlessly as one would tear down a hut in **a garden**. He handed it over to the invaders for destruction, **bringing down in ruins** the **place of meeting** where He had promised to meet with His people. Not a trace of it was left for survivors to use; it was as if He were intent on **wiping out the very memory of festival and Sabbath** sacrifice. The **king**, who had protected it, and the **priest** who ministered there, God utterly **rejected** in His **rage**, dismissing them from His presence. He clearly **despised** the **altar** on which sacrifices to Him were offered and **hated His** own **sanctuary**.

The enemy **made an uproar in the House of Yahweh**, bellowing and hollering as they chopped it up and set it ablaze with the same gusto of previous crowds that had gathered there **on a day of festival**. Yahweh's anger knew no bounds. He **decided to bring down in ruins the wall of the daughter of Zion**, erasing all her protection. He

measured it all **up** carefully with a measuring line, determined not to leave anything standing. He would **not stop until it was** all **destroyed**. How could He do that? Now nothing was left: **Ramparts and walls** all **lay together** on the ground like so much useless rubble, like **dejected** mourners **lamenting** their fate.

The mute rubble and the shattered **gates** with their **bars** spoke of the **king** and the **princes** who also served as the city's protectors. They also could not protect the people, for they were languishing **among the nations**.[5] **The Law was no more** in the land because the priests who transmitted it were dead or deported, and **the prophets** too were gone from sight, for they could **find no vision from Yahweh**. In short, the people had no contact at all with their God, who seemed to have abandoned them and would speak with them no more. What was left to them? The **elders** could only **sit on the ground** (a posture of mourning), overwhelmed, having **sprinkled dust on their heads and put on sackcloth** like those

_____

5   King Jehoiachin had been taken into exile in 597 BC.

mourning the dead. The young people, usually vigorous and optimistic, the hope and future of the nation, were no better off. The young **girls of Jerusalem**, far from looking forward to marriage and family, could only **hang their heads down to the ground** in shame and grief. The total picture is one of devastation and hopelessness.

2:11–19 *Who Will Heal You?*

> ¹¹ My eyes are blind with tears;
>> my stomach churns;
> my heart is spilled on the ground
>> because of the ruin of the daughter of
>>> my people,
> because infants and babies faint
>> in the city streets.
> ¹² They cry to their mothers,
>> "Where is some food?"
> as they faint like a wounded man
>> in the streets of the town,
> as their life is poured out
>> at their mother's breast.

¹³ How can I describe you, to what
    compare you,
      O daughter of Jerusalem?
What plight is like yours, that I may
    comfort you,
      O virgin daughter of Zion?
For your affliction is wide as the sea;
    who can heal you?
¹⁴ Your prophets' visions for you
    were false and bogus;
they have not laid bare your sin
    to save you from exile,
but their visionary oracles for you
    were false and misleading.
¹⁵ All who pass your way
    clap their hands at the sight of you;
they whistle and shake their heads
    at the daughter of Jerusalem:
"Is *this* the city everyone called
    'the perfection of beauty,
the joy of all the earth?'"
¹⁶ All your enemies
    rail against you;

they whistle, grind their teeth,
    and cry: "We have swallowed her!
Ah, this is the day we were waiting for—
    now we've got it, we can see it!"
[17] Yahweh did what he intended;
    he has carried out his word,
which he decreed long ago:
    He has destroyed without pity;
he has made the enemy crow over you
    and made the might of your foes
        triumphant.
[18] Cry from your heart to the Lord,
    to the wall of the daughter of Zion!
Let tears run down like a torrent
    day and night!
Give yourself no rest,
    your eyes no relief!
[19] "Get up, cry out in the nighttime,
    from the early evening!
Pour out your heart like water
    before the Lord's presence!
Lift your hands to him
    for the lives of your children

who faint for hunger
  at the top of every street."

The narrator, whose pain mirrors the pain of the people, now steps forward. The suffering he has witnessed literally turns his **stomach**, which **churns**. His **eyes are blind** from crying uncontrollably; his **heart** (literally "his liver," the seat of emotion) **is spilled** and lies panting **on the ground**. This violent reaction is caused by being forced to witness **infants and babies fainting in the city streets**, in the broad plazas, dying from lack of food. **At their mother's** dry and shrunken **breast**, they find no nourishment and so call **to their mothers** with their dying **cry, "Where is some food?"** (The Living Bible[6] captures it well: "Mamma, mamma, we want food!" Literally, "Where is the grain and the wine?"—i.e., the stored-up supplies formerly available in the marketplace.) Thus the starving children die in their mother's arms.

---

6   Tyndale House Publishers, 1974.

The narrator breaks down as he turns to address the **daughter of Jerusalem**, saying, **"How can I describe you, to what compare you?"** He wants to speak a word of comfort and consolation, tell her that others have endured such things and survived, but he can find nothing to compare with her suffering. **"What plight is like yours?"** he asks. The answer: no one's. No other suffering can compare with yours; **your affliction is wide as the sea**, which to the ancients was an immense, chaotic, and threatening vista. **Who can heal you?** Again, the answer: no one.

The narrator looks back at the cause of the affliction. The court **prophets** were to blame, for their **visions were false and bogus**. They told you what you wanted to hear and did **not lay bare your sin** so that you could have repented and been **saved from exile**. Their **oracles were false and misleading** whitewash coming from their own foolish hearts and not from Yahweh.

Now your ruin is complete and has become one of the wonders of the world. **All who pass your way clap their hands at the sight** of your complete destruction. They mock you, shocked at the change: "**Is this the city everyone called 'the perfection of beauty, the joy of all the earth?'**" Hard to believe! (The references to the city of beauty and joy are from Psalm 50:2 and Psalm 48:2). **All your enemies,** all your surrounding neighbors, join together in a chorus of contempt, **whistling** (an expression of shock) and **grinding their teeth** (an expression of rage) as they **rail against you** and cry, "**We have swallowed her!**" They **waited** long **for** this day of humiliation, and now they cannot contain their joy.

And what can Jerusalem say in reply? How can Jerusalem register a complaint? For **Yahweh did** exactly **what He intended, carrying out the word** of doom He **decreed long ago**. He was the One who made the **enemy crow** and **made the might** (literally "the horn") **of the foe triumphant**. How then could Jerusalem turn to Him for sympathy and help?

Nonetheless, the narrator tells Jerusalem to **cry from** her **heart to the Lord**, to make a scene, to **let tears run down like a torrent** without ceasing, wailing **day and night** without letup. They are to cry out to "**the wall of the daughter of Zion**" (i.e., to the Lord) because He was the true city wall that protected it from invasion and itself.

The time of early evening is usually the time of rest, when the lamps are lit and stories are told. Then comes the nighttime, the time for sleep. But not for you! **Get up, cry out** even **in the nighttime, from the early evening, pouring out your heart's** pain as abundantly as **water** is poured out, humbling yourself **before the Lord's presence. Lift your hands to Him** in prayer, imploring His mercy—if not for you, then mercy **for the lives of your** dying **children. At the top of every street**, they are perishing from **hunger**, with more dying every day.

2:20–22 *Yahweh, Look and See How Terrible It Is!*

²⁰ Look, Yahweh, and see this!
　　Who else have you done this to?
Should women eat their offspring,
　　the children they nurtured?
Should priest and prophet be killed
　　in the Lord's sanctuary?
²¹ In the dust outdoors

lie both young and old;
my girls and my young men
    have fallen by the sword;
you have killed, butchering in the day of
    your rage,
    killing without pity.
²² As though summoning to a festival day,
    you brought
    me terrors from every side,
and on the day of Yahweh's anger
    no one escaped or survived.
Those whom I gave birth to and reared
    my enemy destroyed.

The daughter of Zion finally speaks, doing as she was counseled, and cries from her heart to the Lord (v. 18). It is a cry of almost aggressive accusation. She insists that **Yahweh** open His eyes to **look and see** what He has done. **Who else has** He **done this to?** No one! Does He think it is right that women should be reduced to **eating their offspring** whom they once **nurtured** so lovingly? That **priest and prophet**—who both belong to Him!—should **be killed?** And **in the Lord's** own

sanctuary, no less? If He would but look around, He could see that everywhere **outdoors**, people of all ages, **both young and old,** including **girls and young men** who were the future of the nation, were butchered, now **lying** dead **in the dust**, **killed without pity**. Has He treated any other people so badly? God brought **terrors from every side** upon them as happily as if He were **summoning** people to gather for **a festival day**. There were no **survivors**.

The daughter of Zion ends on the note that keeps coming back to her heart every waking minute: "**Those whom I gave birth to and reared my enemy destroyed.**"[7] Jerusalem's children are dead. That is the accusing cry of the city. But again, Yahweh makes no reply.

---

7   The noun "**enemy**" is here in the singular, not the plural, form. Is she referring to Yahweh?

Second Meditation:
The Suffering of Poverty

They cry to their mothers, "Where is some food?"
(2:12)

MOST WHO ARE READING THESE words have never known true poverty. I remember the observation of the first bishop I served under, Bishop H. V. R. Short (of blessed memory) of the Anglican Diocese of Saskatchewan. He once said to me that if you had breakfast this morning, then you are rich, because many millions of people in the world are only able to eat one meal a day. For them, eating breakfast each day would be an almost unthinkable luxury. By that standard of comparison, this meant almost everyone in Canada is rich—certainly all the people he encountered in the church. His words were a timely reminder of the affluence that we in the West take for granted. That does not mean, I hasten to add, that there are no poor in the West—people who cannot afford to give their children breakfast. That is why some schools offer breakfast programs. But this knowledge does serve to put our Western experience into a more global context.

And into a historical context as well. In most of the world and throughout most of its history, there was nothing that we would recognize as "the middle class." The gap between the rich and the poor was immense. The aristocracy owned fabulous amounts of wealth, and at the other end of the social scale, the peasantry struggled to survive. And then, of course, the slaves owned nothing and could be bought and sold—or killed—at will. There were no social programs to speak of. When the countryside experienced drought or crop failure, thousands starved to death. Life in its natural state was, as the philosopher Thomas Hobbes famously declared, solitary, poor, nasty, brutish, and short. We in the affluent, modern West tend to forget this and expect life in its natural state to be friendly, abundant, happy, civilized, and long—and we are indignant when circumstances are otherwise. The prosperous West is thus set up to misunderstand the nature of poverty.

Admittedly, Bishop Short's wisdom notwithstanding, comparisons are difficult. When children are bullied in school because they are poorer than the other kids, it does not help to inform those kids or their parents that at least they are richer than the children in Haiti or Bangladesh. Poverty is a local matter, and we naturally enough compare ourselves to those around us, not to those on the other side of the globe.

We must ask, therefore, the basic question, "What *is* poverty?" Is it not being able to afford the latest Xbox? Is it not being able to take vacations in Disneyland or Hawaii or China and the Far East? Is it being dependent on food banks? Is it having to work two jobs to pay the bills? Poverty is often defined in terms of need, and the poor are sometimes referred to as "the needy." So, the question becomes, "What do we actually need?"

When one is wealthy and has more than enough of everything, this question never arises, and the advertising industry is at hand to insist that we *need* the latest Xbox or a vacation in Hawaii. But, in fact, we don't *need* these things; we merely *want* them. The wealthy who take long and expensive vacations never really have to face the question of actual need. But the poor do. Their poverty forces them to ask, "What do I actually need?"

It is an important question, and perhaps one of the most basic questions that human beings have to face—and it is to the West's shame that we never really face the question as we should, as developing nations must. Not surprisingly, the Bible has the answer. Saint Paul shared it long ago: "If we have food and clothing, with these we shall be content" (1 Tim. 6:8). That is, if we are warm and fed, that is all we really need.

This does not mean, of course, that we may not aspire to more. We want many things that are good for us: education, health, leisure, and (as St. Paul would insist) the financial resources to give to those in need. It is not wrong to want those good things. It is good to aspire and work hard to get them, although St. Paul again has advice for us when we do—namely, the reminder that the love of money is the source for all kinds of evil (1 Tim. 6:10), so we must take care that greed does not get its hooks into us. But wanting to increase our resources is not wrong.

It is, therefore, a matter of balance. In telling us that we should be content with food and warmth, St. Paul is not trying to limit us or to snuff out ambition. He is taking us back to absolute basics, to ground zero, and reminding us of the human condition. He is reminding us of the big picture and the fact that regardless of how much we accumulate and spend, death will take it all away. "We brought nothing into the world, and we cannot take anything out of the world" (1 Tim. 6:7). As the proverb says, "There are no pockets in a shroud." This big picture can help us put our present difficulties into perspective. Knowing what we are bound for, realizing that we will leave the world naked and penniless, we can understand what we truly and actually need every day: food and shelter. Everything else comes as a gift—superfluous, extra.

And it is just this necessary food and shelter that Christ promises to His disciples. In His Sermon on the Mount, He says to them:

Do not be anxious about your life, what you shall eat or what you shall drink, nor about your body, what you shall put on. Is not life more than food, and the body more than clothing? Look at the birds of the air: they neither sow nor reap nor gather into barns, and yet your heavenly Father feeds them. Are you not of more value than they? And why are you anxious about clothing? Consider the lilies of the field, how they grow; they neither toil nor spin; yet I tell you, even Solomon in all his glory was not arrayed like one of these. But if God so clothes the grass of the field, which today is alive and tomorrow is thrown into the oven, will he not much more clothe you, O men of little faith? Therefore do not be anxious, saying, "What shall we eat?" or "What shall we drink?" or "What shall we wear?" For the Gentiles seek all these things; and your heavenly Father knows that you need them all. But seek first his kingdom and his righteousness, and all these things shall be yours as well. (Matt. 6:25–33)

This, we note, is not a message to the world. Christ is not saying that everyone in the world will be fed and clothed and that starvation will not exist. It is a message to His disciples and His assurance that His Father will look after them. It is His promise that, at the end of the day and by whatever means, including giving us health and strength to work, God will provide us with food and shelter, keeping us warm and fed.

Ultimately our contentment does not—and need not—depend on our financial resources. Saint Paul said that he had learned the secret of getting along with little or a lot. It was this: "I can do all things in him who strengthens me" (Phil. 4:13). If we look to Christ, He will give us peace as He provides for us what we actually need. The strength to which Paul refers is the strength to seek the Kingdom of God regardless of our outer circumstances.

It is a challenging thing to be poor, especially when the poor can see wealthy people all around them. I for one am happy that I live in the West and (as Bishop Short reminded me) am rich enough to eat breakfast every day. But the poor do have this going for them. They have the opportunity to ask and answer the basic question that the wealthy never have to face: What do we actually need? Ultimately, contentment is a choice, as Paul said. We can choose to be content with food and shelter, or we can refuse to be contented until we are playing with our Xbox in Disneyland. There is more to contentment and life than food and shelter. There is seeking the Kingdom of God and His righteousness. Let those who do not know God angst about Xboxes. We, whether poor or well off, have better things to do.

Lamentations Poem Three

3:1–18   The Suffering Sent to God's Servant

¹ I myself am the strong man who has
   seen affliction
   under the rod of his anger;
² he has driven and brought me
   into darkness with no light.
³ Against me alone he turns his hand
   over and over again all day long.
⁴ He has made my flesh and my skin
   waste away
   and broken my bones.
⁵ He has besieged and surrounded me
   with bitterness and hardship.
⁶ He has made me dwell in darkness
   like the dead of long ago.
⁷ He has walled me in; I cannot escape;
   he has made my chain heavy.

[8] Though I cry out and call for help,
    he shuts out my prayer.
[9] He has blocked my ways with cut stones;
    he has made my paths tangled.
[10] He is a bear lying in wait for me,
    a lurking lion.
[11] He dragged me away and tore me to
    pieces;
    he has left me bleeding.
[12] He has bent his bow and taken aim,
    making me a target for his arrow.
[13] He drove into my back
    the arrows of his quiver.
[14] I have become the laughingstock of all
    peoples,[8]
    the target of their abuse all day long.
[15] He has filled me with bitterness;
    he has made me drunk with
    wormwood.

---

8   Masoretic, "my people," singular—i.e., the Hebrew peo-
    ple. If this is the correct reading, it might refer to them
    mocking him for his continued faith in God. About
    fifty Hebrew manuscripts read "peoples" (plural), as
    does the Peshitta (the ancient Syriac version of the Old
    Testament), which uses "the surrounding peoples."

¹⁶ He has made my teeth grind on gravel
    and made me cower in ashes.
¹⁷ Peace is gone from my soul;
    I have forgotten what happiness is,
¹⁸ so I say, "My strength is gone,
    along with my hope from Yahweh."

The poem begins with the voice of a sufferer, one who puts himself forward (in the Hebrew *'ani*, "I" is emphatic) as someone who has **seen** and experienced the **affliction**. He is not a specific individual but the embodiment of the nation's strength and endurance. Although He is a **strong man** (Hebrew *geber*, a different word than *'ish*, the usual word for "man"), his affliction has worn him down.

His enemy (as yet unidentified) seems to be a bad man: He has **driven** him and **brought** him **into darkness with no light**. He has singled out the witness for abuse so that against him **alone** the enemy **turned his hand over and over again all day long,** never resting from giving him a beating. The result? **Flesh and skin** have **wasted away**, **bones broken**. He has kept the speaker caged **in darkness like the dead of long ago**. The enemy **walled** him **in** so that he could find **no escape**, loaded with **a heavy chain** (literally "a heavy bronze," a strong bronze chain). The whole feel is claustrophobic as he speaks about imprisonment and torture. Were all these references, the listener wonders, about the sadistic invading Babylonians?

It is only in verse 8 that the shocking identity of his tormentor is revealed: It is not a Babylonian invader or any mortal man, but God Himself! Though the speaker **cries and calls for help**, we're told, "**he shuts out my prayer**"—the *he* finding its antecedent in the enemy of the previous verses. Yahweh is not absent from the situation: Appallingly, He is the cause of it!

The description of the speaker's suffering continues, made all the more horrific now that we know God is the one inflicting it: God has **blocked** the **ways** of escape **with cut stones** (huge stones, cut for building); the speaker cannot escape from the maze. God is **a bear**; He is **a lion**, **lurking** and **lying in wait** to pounce, **drag away**, **tear to pieces**, and **leave bleeding** and dying his victim. God has **taken aim** with **His bow**; the **arrows of**

His quiver found their **target** in the speaker's **back** (literally "his kidneys"), deep in his body.

Moreover, this man has become a **laughing-stock of all peoples, the target of their abuse all day long**—insults upon injuries! He finds his **teeth grinding on gravel** as he is forced to scavenge for food among the ruins, picking up little stones along with scraps of discarded food. In a culture that emphasizes both shame and honor, he is covered with shame, **cowering in ashes**. In his **soul all peace** has long since departed, along with any memory of **happiness**. He is left to admit to and face what he has long tried not to face: **"My strength is gone, along with my hope from Yahweh."** That reluctant confession is the ultimate cry of despair.

We pause to note that the poem has not yet mentioned the city of Jerusalem and the outrages committed against it. Instead, the speaker has thoroughly internalized the suffering of Judah and Jerusalem, although he will refer to it in verses 42 and following, especially in verse 48. The speaker has become a living metaphor for the national anguish of 586 BC.

3:19–42   *Approaching the God of Mercy*

¹⁹ Remember my anguish and my
      wanderings,
      the wormwood and the gall!
²⁰ My soul constantly remembers it
      and sinks within me.
²¹ But this I call to mind,
      and therefore I have hope:
²² the steadfast love of Yahweh never
      ceases;
      his mercies never come to an end;
²³ they are new every morning.
      Great is your faithfulness!
²⁴ "Yahweh is all that I have," says my soul;
      "therefore I will hope in him."
²⁵ Yahweh is good to those who wait for
      him,
      to the soul who seeks him.
²⁶ It is good that one should wait quietly
      for Yahweh's salvation.
²⁷ It is good for a strong man that he bear
      the yoke in his youth.
²⁸ Let him sit alone in silence
      when it is laid on him;

²⁹ let him put his face in the dust—
    there may yet be hope.
³⁰ Let him give his cheek to the one who
    slaps,
    and let him be filled with insult.
³¹ For the Lord will not
    reject forever,
³² but, though he cause grief, he will have
    compassion
    according to the abundance of his
      steadfast love,
³³ for he takes no pleasure in afflicting
    or punishing any mortal man.
³⁴ To crush underfoot
    all the prisoners of the land,
³⁵ to deny a strong man justice
    in the presence of the Most High,
³⁶ to pervert justice in a lawsuit,
    the Lord never approves.
³⁷ Who has spoken and it was done,
    unless the Lord had commanded it?
³⁸ Is it not from the mouth of the Most
    High
    that both good and bad come?

> ³⁹ Why then should any man living
>   complain, any strong man,
>   about the punishment of his sins?
> ⁴⁰ Let us test and examine our ways,
>   and return to Yahweh!
> ⁴¹ Let us stretch out our hearts and hands
>   to God in heaven:
> ⁴² "We have transgressed and rebelled,
>   and you have not forgiven!"

Then begins this remarkable section, one very different in spirit from the laments that precede and follow it. The speaker cries out to God, **"Remember my anguish and my wanderings**, my homelessness—**my soul constantly remembers it!"** He cannot for a minute forget his sufferings, so he asks God to remember them also. Asking God to "remember" (Hebrew *zakar*) does not mean asking Him simply to recall something mentally but to take action. When God remembers sin, He moves to judge it (see 1 Kings 17:18); the prophetic watchmen who asked God to remember Zion were asking Him to vindicate her (Is. 62:6–7). Here the speaker asks God to save him from his suffering, for when he remembers it, his **soul sinks within** him, and he falls into despair.

But then, unexpectedly, another thought rises up within him—a thought that gives **hope**. It is this: **The steadfast love of Yahweh never ceases; his mercies never come to an end.** Indeed, **they are new every morning**! Excited by this, the speaker cries out to Yahweh, **"Great is Your faithfulness!"** The Hebrew word rendered **"faithfulness"** is *'emunah*, denoting reliability, certainty, integrity.

In this sudden transition from despair to hope, we witness the mysterious, apparent discontinuity that attends all our relationship with God—a discontinuity central to the Book of Job. We know that God is loving, forgiving, merciful, and that His **steadfast love** (Hebrew *hesed*, "covenant love") never fails. Yet even so, we experience things that seem to contradict this, such as sickness, bereavement, and the death of loved ones despite our impassioned and fervent prayers for them—and events such as the destruction of

Jerusalem. There is in our relationship with God and in His rule over the world an element of the incalculable.

The speaker knows this only too well and is faced with a choice of what to believe and how to act. He chooses to believe and trust God, his **soul** concluding, "**Yahweh is all that I have** (literally, "my portion"); **therefore I will hope in him. Yahweh is good to those who wait for him, to the soul who seeks him**." The speaker deliberately turns away from dwelling on his suffering to seek God instead. There is a note of defiance in this decision. Despite all the evidence that God apparently cares nothing for him and will never help him, he chooses to ignore this evidence and to stubbornly trust God. He therefore turns away from tortured analysis of his situation, away from trying to figure out causation, and turns instead to faithful duty. That is, he turns away from the past and sets his face to the future. He recalls that Yahweh was good and merciful in the past with abundant demonstration of His **steadfast love**, so he concludes that He will demonstrate that steadfast love in the future as well.

The upshot? **It is good that one should wait quietly for Yahweh's salvation. It is good for a strong man** (Hebrew *geber*; see v. 1) **that he bear the yoke** of suffering and discipline **in his youth**, letting suffering temper his strength.

The speaker therefore prescribes humility. Let the one suffering **sit alone in silence** when suffering **is laid on him** and not leap up to rant or protest. Let him prostrate humbly before God, **putting his face** (literally "his mouth") **in the dust**, trusting that **there may yet be hope**. When life **slaps** him, let him **give his cheek** willingly and accept the insult, not offer violent retaliation to recover his honor.[9] He trusts that humility will have its reward, **for the Lord will not reject** his prayer **forever** but will eventually **have compassion according to the abundance of His steadfast love**.

Such a decision builds confidence in his soul about God's goodness. He therefore declares that God **takes no pleasure in afflicting or punishing**

---

9   In that culture, a slap was not considered an assault as it is in our culture but rather an insult to one's honor.

any mortal man (literally He "does not afflict from His heart," the heart being the organ of volition and decision). Terrible things are done by men—**prisoners of the land** are **crushed underfoot**, **strong men** (Hebrew *geber*) are **denied justice** as the wicked prosper, **justice** in lawsuits **is perverted** through bribery. The earth is full of such outrages, and of such **the Lord never approves**.

But God clearly allows this wrongdoing, for **is it not from the mouth of the Most High** who governs all that happens on earth **that both good and bad come?** God knows what He is doing. **Why** then **should any man living** (Hebrew *'adam*), **any strong man** (Hebrew *geber*), **complain about the punishment of his sins?** Sinners like us, however mighty and self-sufficient, should trust God's goodness. Rather than judge and condemn Yahweh, we should **test and examine our** own **ways** and **return to Yahweh** in penitence. We should **stretch out our hearts** as well as our **hands** (stretching out the hand was the ancient posture for prayer) and cry **to God in heaven**, "We **have transgressed and rebelled, and you have not forgiven!"**

3:43–66   *Prayer for Vindication*

43 "You have wrapped yourself in anger
    and pursued us,
    butchering without pity.
44 You have hidden yourself behind the
    clouds
    so that no prayer can pass through.
45 You have made us filth and rubbish
    among the peoples.
46 "All our enemies
    open their mouths against us.
47 Panic and pitfall have come upon us,
    devastation and destruction!
48 My eyes run with rivers of tears
    because of the destruction of the
    daughter of my people.
49 "My eyes will stream without letup,
    without relief,
50 until Yahweh from heaven
    looks down and sees.
51 My eyes grow sore
    at the fate of all the daughters of
        my city.

> ⁵²"I have been hunted like a bird
>   by those who were my enemies
>   without cause;
> ⁵³ they flung me alive into the cistern
>   and threw stones at me;
> ⁵⁴ water closed over my head;
>   I said, 'I am lost!'"

Armed with hope, the narrator continues his prayer, first stating his people's plight: God had seemingly **wrapped Himself in anger and pursued** them, **butchering** with the sword of Babylon **without pity**. He was deaf to their cries for help, having **hidden** Himself far away **behind the clouds** of heaven, far from their **prayers**. His neglect made them like **filth and rubbish among the peoples**, garbage to be thrown away—so little did He think of the daughters of Zion and Judah! **Panic and pitfall** (a phrase with alliteration and assonance in the Hebrew: *pachad* and *wapachat*) **came upon them**, terror and a trap.

Because of this the narrator's eyes **will stream** tears **without letup until Yahweh from heaven looks down and sees**. This constant weeping makes his **eyes sore**. Note well that here Yahweh is no longer the one destroying them but is looking on from afar as others destroy them.

The narrator's complaint continues: He has been **hunted like a** helpless, fleeing **bird**. Using a new metaphor, he sees himself as a captured animal, **flung alive into the cistern** and stoned. Again, he shifts to another metaphor: He is like a drowning man, with **water closing over** his **head**. His last words as he drowns are "**I am lost!**" The rapid variety of images reflects his mounting panic.

> [55] "I called on your name, Yahweh,
> from the bottom of the pit;
> [56] you heard my plea, 'Do not turn a deaf ear
> to my cry for help!'
> [57] You drew near when I called on you;
> you said, 'Do not fear!'
> [58] "You have taken up my cause, O Lord;
> you have redeemed my life.
> [59] You have seen the wrong done to me, Yahweh;
> give me justice!

⁶⁰ You have seen all their vengeance,
　　all their plots against me!
⁶¹ "You have heard their abuse, Yahweh,
　　all their plots against me.
⁶² The words and schemes of my attackers
　　are against me all the day long.
⁶³ Look at them! Whether sitting or rising,
　　I am the object of their abuse!
⁶⁴ "You will repay them, Yahweh,
　　according to what they have done.
⁶⁵ You will give them hardness of heart;
　　your curse will be on them.
⁶⁶ Pursue them in anger and destroy them
　　from under your heavens, Yahweh!"

Then comes the hoped-for vindication: The speaker has **called on Yahweh's name** (invoked His power), even **from the bottom of the pit** when all hope seemed gone, and heard His welcome response, "**Do not fear!**" The Lord has finally **taken up** his **cause** and **redeemed** his **life**, buying him back from death. Now the speaker cries for **justice**, for vengeance. **Yahweh has seen** all the **wrong done** to him, **all their plots**. He has **heard** their **abuse** and their **words and schemes** against him. Let Him now take action!

The speaker can hardly contain his indignation at them—just **look at them**, Yahweh! **Sitting** down at ease or **rising** up to carry out their plots, **I am the object of their abuse**! Their malevolence never rests. May Yahweh **harden their hearts** so that they carry on and finally receive His **curse**!

This strong man ends on a note of imprecation: "**Pursue them in anger and destroy them from under your heavens, Yahweh!**" Let not a trace of them remain! This is not the voice of vindictiveness but of helplessness in the face of injustice, the voice of pain, the voice of all oppressed generations, the voice of those whose only hope for justice lies with God.

Third Meditation:
The Suffering of Bereavement

My eyes run with rivers of tears because of the destruction of the daughter of my people. (3:18)

IT IS EASY TO QUOTE the line "No man is an island" from the poem by John Donne; it is not as easily recognized that his proverb contains a note of doom. Donne correctly noted that we are all connected to each other, so that "any man's death diminishes me / Because I am involved in mankind."[10] The note of doom sounds when we face not the death of "any man" but the death of someone close to us, someone we love, like a spouse, a sibling, or a child.

---

10   John Donne, "No Man Is an Island," in *The Complete Poetry and Selected Prose of John Donne*, ed. Charles M. Coffin (Modern Library, 2001), 421.

We need a poet like Donne to remind us that anyone's death diminishes us and that their death is in some way our own, that the death's bell, whenever it tolls, is tolling for us. But we need no such reminder that we are diminished when a loved one dies. In that case, we are not just "diminished"; in that case, a part of us dies and is buried with them. We find it hard to leave the gravesite after the burial, to go on with our life—a life from which they have so completely vanished. Rising the next day and carrying on is difficult after the death of a spouse, even if the couple has shared a long life together. It is infinitely harder after the death of a child. Everyone feels that such a death is unnatural. It is as Théoden said of his slain son, Théodred, in Peter Jackson's movie *The Two Towers*: "No parent should have to bury their child."[11]

I am happy to say that thus far in my life I have never had to experience something as traumatic and crippling as the death of a spouse or a child. People who *have* experienced it speak to the rest of

---

11 *The Lord of the Rings: The Two Towers*, directed by Peter Jackson (New Line Cinema, 2002).

us from what seems to be another planet. We can scarcely understand anything the bereaved say or know anything of what they feel.

Moreover, sometimes we don't want to know. The very presence of the bereaved is too vivid a reminder of what awaits us all. Death is not a misfortune like bankruptcy or paralysis from a stroke—something terrible but also something we might not experience. No. Death comes to all; it is "the covering that is cast over all peoples, the veil that is spread over all the nations" (Is. 25:7). The Scriptures are clear: "It is appointed for men to die once" (Heb. 9:27), and none can avoid or dodge that appointment. Fear of death—a fear we can either face or refuse to face—is the fundamental and defining fact of human existence. Animals, so far as we can tell, do not fear death. For them, death is not a tragedy but merely the closing of a circle, the natural end, the way it's supposed to be.

Not so for us. For human beings, death is a fundamental contradiction of our humanity, an obscenity, the way it's *not* supposed to be. For us, death is an enemy, a monster. How much more do we feel its monstrosity when it comes to claim a loved one!

What can we do when faced with bereavement? What can we say?

The first thing perhaps is for us to acknowledge that bereavement separates the recently bereaved from the rest of us, especially from those who have never suffered it. One man who suffered bereavement testified that the voices of his friends could hardly reach him, that the pain of loss formed a kind of wall dividing him from his friends and well-wishers. He also said how surprised he was that grief felt so much like fear.[12] In our interactions with the bereaved, this separation must be recognized.

Also, we should resist the temptation to try to alleviate the suffering of the bereaved by *explaining*. It is a natural thing to do, especially for Christians. We want to reach out and help, and we imagine that if we could only find a good and convincing explanation for why the person died, it would somehow lessen the grief.

---

12   The reference is to C. S. Lewis in his autobiographical book *A Grief Observed* (Seabury Press, 1961).

I am told this is not so; explanations do *not* help. The bereaved do not want to have explained to them that it was all for the best or that the departed are "in a better place." They do not want to have St. Paul's words rammed down their throats that "in everything God works for good" (Rom. 8:28). Such proffered explanations, though well-intentioned, are often offered to help the one who says them cope with their sense of awkwardness and helplessness as much as to help the bereaved. Best not to try to explain.

What might help the bereaved? Pain and grief cannot be diluted with explanation, but they can be shared—most often by simple embrace and silence. Silence? Yes, silence, for what can one say to a friend after they bury their child? Tears also are appropriate: Christ wept at the grave of His friend Lazarus even though He knew He would soon raise him up (John 11:35). And St. Paul told us to "weep with those who weep" (Rom. 12:15). It is often and truly said that a joy shared is doubled and a grief shared is halved—or, at least, somewhat lessened for a moment's respite.

Ultimately, bereavement is a suffering that finds no solace in this age, a question that has no answer, a fishhook that remains lodged in the heart until the heart ceases to beat. When the one who died was close, such as a spouse or a child, one never really "gets over it." Time does not heal all wounds.

But eternity does. Or, more precisely, Christ heals the wounds of bereavement in eternity, in heaven, in the age to come. That is why, to reference a quote often attributed to C. S. Lewis, Christians never say "goodbye," for Christians are never finally separated from one another. They only say "au revoir" or "I'll be seeing you," for they will meet again and finally find each other in the Kingdom.

In this age we carry the pain of bereavement all our days, just as we carry our own mortality through all our days in the form of ill health, periodic sickness, or tragedy. We know that we will always struggle with sickness and that eventually sickness will win out, and we will die. In this life, bereavement and mortality walk hand in hand. But Christ has trampled down death by His own death, and our mortality will not have the last word. Christ will.

And that last word will be a word of joy, of immortality, of deathless joy and sunlit triumph. In this life we walk through the valley of the shadow of death, a vale of tears, and many of those tears are the tears of bereavement. In the age to come, Christ has promised to wipe away all our tears, including the tears of those who have suffered loss.

The psalmist had it right: "Weeping may tarry for the night, / but joy comes with the morning" (Ps. 30:5). In the long night of this life, we suffer and grieve. But the morning is coming, and with it, a day that will know no evening.

We have all enjoyed looking at scenes of happy reunion, especially when someone long separated from a loved one is surprised by their unexpected return. We enjoy seeing how they run into each other's embrace, wrapping arms and sometimes even legs around them in rapturous reunion. That is what awaits all the bereaved in the Kingdom. It is the ultimate and only answer to their present suffering. We wait with patience throughout this long and terrible night. Joy comes in the morning.

Lamentations Poem Four

4:1–11 *The Horrors of the Siege*

> ¹ Ah, how the gold has tarnished,
>   how the pure gold is dulled!
> The holy stones now lie scattered
>   at every street corner.
> ² The precious sons of Zion,
>   worth their weight in fine gold,
> how they are regarded as no better than
>   earthen pots,
>   made by a potter!

The poem opens with an impossibility—namely, the **tarnishing** and **dulling** of **gold**. Pure gold, of course, cannot tarnish—and that is the point. It was also thought impossible that Jerusalem, the city protected by the living God of Israel, could be penetrated and fall, but so it happened. Zion's golden and glorious past, a past filled with divine favor, had come to an inglorious end. The **holy stones** of the temple, once magnificently aligned and placed together to form the sacred edifice, now lay separated and **scattered at every street corner**, like worthless rubble.

The precious temple stones image **the precious sons of Zion**, **worth their weight in gold**—children who were the true gold and the true treasures of Zion. They also have tarnished. Though precious, they now **are regarded as no better than** common **earthen pots** made by a common **potter**—easily made, easily broken, easily discarded. In the siege and fall of Jerusalem, the sons were broken and killed or sold into slavery.

> ³ Even jackals offer the breast;
>   they suckle their young,
> but the daughter of my people has grown
>   cruel,
>   like the ostriches in the desert.
> ⁴ The tongue of the nursing infant sticks
>   to its palate for thirst;
> the children beg for food,

but no one gives them any.
⁵ Those who once fed on delicacies
    perish in the streets;
those who were brought up in scarlet
    grovel on rubbish heaps.

During the siege, the narrator relates that **the daughter of** his **people** had seemingly **grown cruel**. **Jackals** and **ostriches**, proverbially care-less of their young, at least care for their offspring enough to make sure they are fed. The jackal **offers the breast to suckle** her **young** and doesn't let them go hungry. But not Jerusalem—she didn't feed her young but let them starve to death. **The tongue of the nursing infant** would **stick to its palate for thirst**, unable to find drink. **The chil-dren** would leave the house to **beg for food, but no one gave them** anything. They and their families **once fed on delicacies** in their houses, but now they **perish** from hunger outside **in the streets**. They were **brought up in scarlet**, rolling in luxury (compare Prov. 31:21); now they **grovel** on the ground **on rubbish heaps**, scrounging for any food they can find. In this way the speaker emphasizes the horrors of the siege, which left infants and children starving. Animals fed their young, but Jerusalem did not feed hers—because she couldn't.

> [6] For the crime of the daughter of my
> people has been greater
> than the sin of Sodom,
> which was overthrown in a moment
> with no time to wring the hands.
> [7] Her princes were purer than snow,
> whiter than milk;
> their bodies were rosier than coral,
> their limbs like sapphire.
> [8] Now their faces are blacker than soot;
> they are unrecognizable in the streets.
> Their skin has shriveled on their bones,
> dry as a stick.
> [9] More fortunate were the victims of the
> sword
> than the victims of hunger
> who wasted away, pierced
> by lack of the produce of the field.
> [10] The hands of tenderhearted women

have boiled their own children;
they became their gruel
during the smashing of the daughter
of my people.
¹¹ Yahweh gave full vent to his wrath;
he poured out his hot anger,
and he kindled a fire in Zion
that devoured its foundations.

All this involuntary cruelty was rooted in crime,
the crime of rebellion against God. Indeed, **the
crime** of Jerusalem was **greater** than the prover-
bial **sin of Sodom**, whose sins were so appalling
that it was **overthrown in a moment with no time**
for anyone watching **to wring** their **hands** over
them. With such a great and rebellious sin, no
wonder Jerusalem suffered so much!

The judgment on Jerusalem's sin could be
seen in the bodies of **her princes**. Once their
faces were **purer than snow, whiter than milk**—
happy and radiant countenances. **Their bodies** were ruddy with health, **rosier than coral,
their limbs like sapphire**—the picture of perfect
strength and vitality. Now they were starving

and sick, their faces dark with the ravages of hunger, **blacker than soot, unrecognizable** by their friends when met **in the streets**. Their **skin** had **shriveled on their bones**, as **dry** and dehydrated **as a** dead **stick**.

The narrator offers this analysis of the terrible situation: **More fortunate than these were the victims of the sword**, those cut down and now dead. Better to be dead than to be the victims of famine, **wasting away**, **pierced** not by a sword but by the pains of hunger caused **by lack of the produce of the field**. The piecing pain of the sword lasts only a moment before death comes; the piercing pain of hunger goes on and on.

The narrator now reveals just how intolerable that pain was when he says that it caused even **the hands of tender-hearted women** to kill and **boil their own children** in their desperation to find something to eat. These young ones, perhaps the first to die because of their youth, **became gruel** for their starving parents **during the smashing of the daughter of my people**. The word rendered *gruel* here translates the Hebrew *barah*, a different word than the usual word for food, meaning

the diet intended for a sick person. Thus did **Yahweh give full vent to His wrath, kindling a fire
in Zion** so hot and out of control that it **devoured**
Zion down to **its** very **foundations**.

4:12–20 *The Results of the Siege*

> ¹²The kings of the earth could not believe,
>   nor any of the inhabitants of the world,
> that the enemy or invader could penetrate
>   the gates of Jerusalem.
> ¹³This was for the sins of her prophets
>   and the crimes of her priests,
> who shed in her midst
>   the blood of the righteous.
> ¹⁴They wandered blindly through the
>   streets
>   so stained with blood
> that no one would touch
>   their garments.
> ¹⁵ "Away! Unclean!" the people cried to
>   them.
>   "Away! Away! Don't touch us!"
> So they became fugitives and wanderers;

> people said among the nations,
> "They can't stay here either."
> ¹⁶ Yahweh himself has scattered them;
>   he gave them not a thought,
> showing no honor to the priests,
>   no favor to the elders.

The fall of Jerusalem came as a shock to **the kings of the earth**. They had doubtless heard some of the songs of Zion (see Ps. 137:3) celebrating the land as "the perfection of beauty" (Ps. 50:2) and could scarcely take in what had happened to it. Nor could any of **the inhabitants of the world**. People high and low simply could not believe it. They could not believe that **the enemy or invader could penetrate the gates of Jerusalem** that Judah declared were guarded by none other than their God Himself. How could it happen?

It happened, the narrator explains, **for the sins of her prophets and the crimes of her priests.** The prophets refused to warn Jerusalem of her sins. Instead, they prophesied that all was well and all would be well. The priests connived this way as well, allowing idolatrous worship to flourish even within the confines of the temple (see Ez. 8). All of them, prophets and priests, allowed the wicked to **shed the blood of the righteous** in the very **midst** of the city through injustice. The whole system was compromised, from top to bottom.

Judgment therefore had to fall upon them. Just as touching blood made one ritually unclean, so shedding the blood of the righteous made the religious leaders spiritually unclean. They are portrayed as lepers, **wandering blindly through the streets**, not allowed in anyone's home because of their uncleanness. **No one would** even **touch** the **garments** of those so unclean. They **cried to them** as one would shout at lepers, "**Away! Unclean! Don't touch us!**" So they went into exile as **fugitives and wanderers**, people utterly without help, ally, or hope; even **among the nations** they were rejected and found no rest. The foreign nations didn't want them living there and said **among** themselves, "**They can't stay here either.**"

Thus did **Yahweh Himself** (literally "the face of Yahweh," for the verdict came straight from Him) **scatter them** without **giving them a** further **thought**. He **showed no honor to the priests**, no

favor to the elders of the people, even though priests and elders in that culture traditionally were treated with respect. Out they went, worthless criminals that they were. They could live or die among the nations; Yahweh didn't care.

> ¹⁷ Still we strained our eyes, ever watching
>   vainly for help.
> We watched and kept on watching
>   for a nation that could not save us
>   anyway.
> ¹⁸ They harried our steps
>   so that we could not walk in our streets.
> Our end was near, our days numbered;
>   our end had come.
> ¹⁹ Our pursuers were swifter
>   than the eagles in the sky;
> they chased us on the mountains;
>   they lurked for us in the desert.
> ²⁰ Our very life, Yahweh's anointed,
>   was captured in their pits,
> of whom we boasted, "Under his shadow
>   we shall live safely among the
>   nations!"

Then come, somewhat suddenly, the voices of survivors. They come with their horrifying testimony of the last days. They relate the desperate hope to which they clung during the siege: **Still we strained our eyes, ever watching vainly for help**, **watching** day and night (literally "on our watchtowers we watched") **for a nation** (they bitterly say) **that could not save us anyway**. (Egypt was the ally on which they were counting for help.) When the final attack came, the enemy **harried their steps** so that they **could not walk in their streets**, in the open squares. They were forced to flee through hidden byways as they sought escape. One can still hear the heartbreaking resignation in the voices of these people many centuries later: **"Our end was near, our days numbered; our end had come."** Their invading **pursuers were swifter than eagles in the sky**, swooping down suddenly on their helpless prey. Death above, coming from the sky; death also here below, **on the mountains and in the desert**. Death everywhere.

Even their **very life** (literally "the breath of our nostrils"), **Yahweh's anointed**, King Zedekiah, could not save them. He **was captured in their**

pits along with the rest of his army. This was the one **of whom** they **boasted, "Under his shadow** and protection **we shall live safely among the nations."** He turned out to be a false hope. Nothing and no one could save them.

4:21–22   *The Vengeance on Edom*

> ²¹ Rejoice and be glad, O daughter of Edom,
>   as you dwell in the land of Uz;
> but the cup shall pass to you too;
>   you shall become drunk and expose
>   yourself.
> ²² The punishment of your iniquity,
>   O daughter of Zion, is now complete;
>   he will keep you in exile no longer;
> but your iniquity, O daughter of Edom, he
>   will punish;
>   he will uncover your sins.

After recounting the terrible results of the siege of Jerusalem, the narrator turns not to God but to **the daughter of Edom**, Jerusalem's neighbor to the southeast. They were racial kin as well as geographical neighbors, so help, or at least sympathy, might have been expected. Not at all! Rather, Edom aided the invaders, taking delight in Jerusalem's destruction and cutting down her fleeing refugees. For the time being, the narrator ironically tells them, **rejoice and be glad** and **dwell** securely **in the land of Uz**—but, he adds, your day will come. **The cup** of reeling that we were made to drink will **pass to you too**. You too will drink and **become drunk and expose yourself** as drunkards do, bearing God's wrath and the shame of defeat. **The punishment** for the **iniquity of the daughter of Zion is now complete** with their **exile**, and the day for **punishing the daughter of Edom** is still to come. But come it will. God will **uncover** their **sins** soon enough.

Jerusalem takes what little comfort it can. Their solace lies in the thought that God's justice is not reserved for them alone. Their enemy next door will suffer His justice as well.

Fourth Meditation:
The Suffering of Sickness

Their skin has shriveled on their bones, dry as a stick. (4:8)

IT IS CUSTOMARY TO TALK about "sickness and death," those archenemies of the human race, as if they are two separate things. In truth, they are one. Death, or mortality, is *the* fundamental fact about humanity, the condition affecting and infecting us all. Sickness, or disease, is simply its main symptom.

We all have the "disease" of mortality, and we all suffer in varying degrees from the symptoms of this sickness. As we age, the normal progression is for the symptoms to grow worse until the disease finally claims us and we die. Admittedly, we might avoid most of mortality's symptoms if we die young, perhaps in a car accident or murdered in an alley but, happily, that is not likely. Most of us will live well into adulthood and old age and find that sickness is a part of our aging that ends with our death. As my dad wryly and philosophically observed after being diagnosed with cancer in his old age, "Well, you gotta die from something."

Sickness can be defined narrowly or broadly—that is, we can use the term narrowly to denote temporary diseases or ailments such as a cold, a flu, an infection, or, more alarmingly, cancer. The question "Are you sick?" then means, "Are you suffering from a temporary ailment or disease?" By this definition, where sickness is a regrettable and unpleasant interlude in a life of health, it is possible not to be sick.

Or the term *sickness* can be used more broadly, as I am using it here. That is, it can include not just acute diseases but also chronic conditions such as birth defects like spina bifida or congenital deafness, seasonal allergies, glaucoma, diabetes, a weak heart, hardening of the arteries, clinical depression, schizophrenia, and Lewy body dementia, among a host of others. In other words, the term *sickness* can be used to describe the human condition of weakness and mortality that eventually leads to death. By this definition, we are all sick in one way or another because we are all mortal and vulnerable. And terminal.

Saint Paul referred to this condition as living in a "lowly body" (*soma tes tapeinoseos* in Greek; literally the "body of our humiliation"), and he contrasted it with the "glorious body" that we will receive at the resurrection on the Last Day when Christ returns for His Second Coming (Phil. 3:21). Paul also observed that "our outer nature is wasting away," and he contrasted that with "our inner nature," which "is being renewed" day by day (2 Cor. 4:16). This process of slow decay is what I mean by "sickness."

So, to the question, "Father Lawrence, are you sick?" I would answer (at the risk of citing Monty Python), "Yes, of course, but I'm not dead yet." The answer reminds one of the old children's rhyme: "Doctor, doctor, will I die? Yes, my child, and so will I." We are all sick, and will all die. But, my child, happily not yet!

When one sees that suffering and sickness are a part of the human condition, this understanding can serve to put our suffering into perspective. It is now no longer a matter of *if* I will be sick or well—as if sickness could be avoided—but rather of *how* sick I am and of how quickly the sickness will bring me to my end. My sickness is presupposed either way.

We can also see why Christ healed sicknesses. His miracles of healing were not simply signs He performed to impress and wow as proof that He was divine. Christ came to liberate us from sin *and* death and to bestow forgiveness, sonship, and eternal life. He came to die, to trample down death by His own death. He came, ultimately, to bestow immortality upon us and transform our mortal bodies into immortal bodies—bodies no longer sick or subject to death. That is why He performed miracles of healing. His long war against death involved intermediate skirmishes with sickness. The final victory against sickness and death will have to wait until the Last Day—though even before that, Christ sometimes offers a foretaste of the final triumph. Either way, we are all sick, and we will all be healed. But for that final healing, we will have to wait.

Here in this age our bodies are perishable and so will sicken and die. But at the final resurrection we will be changed in the blink of an eye so that our perishable selves put on imperishability (1 Cor. 15:54). Then our bodies will no longer be subject to death. Death (i.e., sickness) will no longer have dominion over us because we will then be like Christ, and "death no longer has dominion over Him" (Rom. 6:9). When we die, our bodies will be sown in the earth in weakness and dishonor, but they will later be raised in power and glory (1 Cor. 15:43).

Sickness should not be minimized or dismissed as if it were nothing. It is suffering indeed, especially when it involves pain and the slow and heartbreaking erosion of our natural faculties, such as with Lewy body dementia or Lou Gehrig's disease. But even then, Paul has something to say: "This slight momentary affliction is preparing for us an eternal weight of glory beyond all comparison, because we look not to the things that are seen but to the things that are unseen; for the things that are seen are transient, but the things that are unseen are eternal" (2 Cor. 4:17–18).

How, we may ask, could we say that a disease like Lou Gehrig's is a "slight momentary affliction"? Precisely because it is momentary and temporal compared with the eternity of joy that awaits us after only a few decades on earth. As is well said and sung in the hymn "Amazing Grace": "When we've been there ten thousand years, bright shining as the sun, we've no less days to sing God's praise, than when we first begun."

The suffering of sickness will end, and our decaying outer body will be sown in dust. Our inner nature can rejoice even now despite the decay, for a new outer nature awaits us at the resurrection, raised in power, raised in glory, and drenched in joy. Knowing this, we may begin to sing God's praise even now.

Lamentations Poem Five

5:1–18   Zion's Plea for Help

¹ Remember, Yahweh, what has befallen us;
   see, look at our disgrace!
² Our inheritance has been turned over to
   strangers,
   our homes to foreigners.
³ We are orphans, fatherless;
   our mothers are like widows.
⁴ We must pay for the water we drink;
   the firewood we get must be bought.
⁵ We are persecuted;
   we are worked to death, given no rest.
⁶ We hold out our hand to Egypt and to
   Assyria
   to get enough bread.
⁷ Our fathers sinned and are gone;
   we bear the burden of their iniquities.

⁸ Slaves rule over us;
    there is none to rescue us from their
    hand.
⁹ We risk our lives to earn a living
    because of the desert sword.
¹⁰ Our skin is hot as an oven
    with the burning heat of famine.
¹¹ Women are raped in Zion,
    girls in the towns of Judah.
¹² Princes are hung up by their hands;
    no respect is shown to the elders.
¹³ Young men are compelled to grind at
    the mill,
    and boys stagger under loads of
      firewood.
¹⁴ The old men have abandoned the city
    gate,
    the young men their music.

The final poem begins with a plea that **Yahweh remember what has befallen** them—that He take action to restore them. As an encouragement to Him, the narrator paints a picture of life after Jerusalem's fall, after their **homes** had **been turned over to strangers** and **foreigners**.

Some children are **orphans, fatherless**, their fathers slaughtered by the invaders; some **mothers**, the women whose husbands were deported, **are like widows**. The very necessities of life that they used to gather freely—**water** to **drink, firewood** to warm them—must now **be bought** from the invaders. The people find themselves **persecuted** (literally "pursued on our necks"), yoked, and **worked to death, given no rest**. They are humiliated, forced to **hold out** their **hands** like beggars **to get enough bread** to eat, begging even from their ancient foes, **Egypt** and **Assyria**. This reference is to any of the superpowers to the south and north, not specifically to Egypt and Assyria, for by then Assyria was no longer in existence, neither politically nor militarily.

Jerusalem's people keenly feel the injustice of it all, as if they are suffering for the misdeeds of the previous generation: Their **fathers sinned and** now **are gone**, swept away to death, and they alone remain to **bear the burden** of their fathers'

iniquities. Worse yet, **slaves** now **rule over** them. The reference to slaves might refer to their new masters' slaves, who domineer over them in their masters' names, or it might refer to the puppet government the oppressors installed—or both. Either way, slaves were utterly unsuited to the task of ruling.

The picture is one of a complete breakdown of society and infrastructure, a picture of chaos and danger. Violent men—gangs—oppress the innocent, destroying and stealing crops, while the people **risk** their **lives** in the fields **to earn a living** because of the oppressors' **desert sword**. Yet the gangs steal their food, leaving them with nothing, so that their **skin is hot as an oven with the burning heat of famine**. **Women are raped in** the city of **Zion**, calling out in vain for help; the young **girls in the towns** and villages are also violated (compare Deut. 22:25–27). **Princes**, those who were once rich and respected, whom no one would dare touch, now are **hung up by their hands** when interrogated. **Elders** who formerly ruled are **shown no respect**. Strong **young men are compelled to grind at the mill**, performing onerous, menial, and degrading labor; young **boys stagger under loads of firewood**, doing the work of slaves.

All life has turned topsy-turvy. Little wonder that **old men have abandoned** their customary positions of honor at **the city gate** and **young men** no longer make **music**, as was customary in former days. The social breakdown has affected everything and everyone, both young and old, both men and women. No good thing has been left untouched. Nothing normal is left.

> [15] The joy has ceased from our hearts;
>   our dancing has been turned into
>   mourning.
> [16] The garland has fallen from our head;
>   woe to us, for we have sinned!
> [17] This is why our hearts have become sick;
>   this is why our eyes have grown dim:
> [18] Mount Zion lies desolate;
>   jackals prowl in it.

In short, **joy** had **ceased from** all their **hearts**, their **dancing turned into mourning**. The festal **garland**, worn during times of joy such as weddings, had **fallen from** their **head**, never to be restored. Their **hearts** were **sick**, their **eyes dim**. They were exhausted and numb. **Mount Zion**, the noisy, bustling, thriving city, once celebrated as safe and impregnable, the joy of the whole earth, now **lies desolate**, abandoned, ruined, uninhabitable. **Jackals prowl in it** to scavenge for food.

5:19–22   *A Final Cry*

> ¹⁹ But you, Yahweh, reign forever;
>   your throne endures to all generations.
> ²⁰ Why do you forget us forever;
>   why do you forsake us these many days?
> ²¹ Turn us back to yourself, Yahweh, and
>   we will come back!
>   Renew our days like in old times.
> ²² Or have you truly rejected us?
>   Will you always be angry with us?

The poem ends on a note of faith, looking beyond the present suffering to the throne of **Yahweh**, where He rules over all nations and **reigns forever**. But the narrator's faith in Yahweh also carries a question: If Yahweh, their nation's God, is truly all-powerful and can overthrow Babylon, **why** is it that He **forgets** them as He does and **forsakes them these many days?** If only He would **turn** them **back** to Himself, restoring them to favor, **renewing** their nation's life **like in old times**, as it was before! Will He not do this? Is it because He has finally and **truly rejected** them? **Will** He **always** be this **angry**?

With this question the poem—and the book—ends. No answer is given. The question hangs in the air, pointing to the future.

Fifth Meditation:
The Suffering of Persecution

We are persecuted; we are worked to death, given no rest. (1:5)

STRANGE AS IT MAY SOUND to people living in the recently Christian West or in the American Bible Belt, persecution is the world's natural and instinctive response to the Christian Faith. Persecution, of course, varies in intensity and consistency. It can range from minor persecution—such as being unpopular with friends and coworkers when they discover our Christian Faith or when we openly espouse Christian views—to heavy persecution, including arrest, imprisonment, beating, torture, and even execution in places such as China, Saudi Arabia, and the former Soviet Union. Indeed, those who have experienced the latter are tempted to deny the term *persecution* to the former. "Being *unpopular* with the crowd? You call that persecution? Let me show you my scars . . ." Still, what all forms of persecution have in common is the fact that openly and boldly confessing discipleship to Jesus Christ and contradicting the world brings retaliation.

It always has. As early as our Lord's earthly ministry, discipleship to Him came at a cost: "The Jews had already agreed that if anyone should confess him to be Christ, he was to be put out of the synagogue" (John 9:22). The Lord Himself predicted such a cost during His final night with His disciples when He said: "Remember the word that I said to you, 'A servant is not greater than his master.' If they persecuted me, they will persecute you; if they kept my word, they will keep yours also . . . The hour is coming when whoever kills you will think he is offering service to God" (John 15:20, 16:2). The Master's words find an echo in St. Paul in his words to Timothy: "All who desire to live a godly life in Christ Jesus will be persecuted" (2 Tim. 3:12).

And so it was. The apostles were persecuted by the Jews after the day of Pentecost and then, all too soon, by the Gentile Romans as well. After the Great Fire of Rome in AD 64, Emperor Nero looked about for scapegoats. By then, Christians were already hated, making them the perfect victims. Eventually the persecution of Christians became government policy and remained so until Constantine called off the dogs of war in AD 313.

Then came the long and glorious "blip" that was Byzantium, when the Roman State did not wage war upon Christians but favored them. (Hindsight eventually saw that such favor proved to be a mixed blessing.) Byzantium in the East and Christendom in the West meant that for hundreds of years, there was no persecution of the Church.

As anyone can see, Byzantium is now dead, and Western Christendom has crumbled, leaving behind only pockets of the Christian Faith in the midst of increasingly secular societies. And the pace of militant secularization seems to be picking up. Those alive in the 1950s in North America can scarcely recognize their world in 2025. We can, I gloomily suggest, expect an increase of unpopularity for Christians in the West in the decades to come. Christians are even now unpopular and violently persecuted in China and in Islamic countries, but their persecution and plight are gravely underreported by the Western media. Such underreporting is in itself a form of persecution. One wonders if there are some who deliberately want to deny Christians sympathy from society at large.

One wants to ask, Why? Why are Christians so unpopular? Why have they been hated from the time of Christ? Why are they violently targeted even now in many parts of the world? Given the Christian track record for doing good (e.g., opening medical clinics and operating social programs to feed the hungry), you would guess that Christians would be *popular*, not *un*popular. But so it is.

One could put forward many sociological, psychological, and historical reasons, but the ultimate reason is spiritual—or, to be more precise, *eschatological*, having to do with the eschatological character of the time since the death, Resurrection, and Ascension of Christ. The "last days" began with the day of Pentecost (see Acts 2, which describes the Pentecostal outpouring as taking place "in the last days"). With Christ the final act of human history has begun so that St. Paul spoke of those living in his time as those "upon whom the end of the ages has come" (1 Cor. 10:11). Saint John said the same: "Children, it is the last hour" (1 John 2:18). It is in this last hour that the final battle of light and darkness is being fought.

We see this dimension of our current age revealed in the Book of Revelation. In Revelation 12:7–12, we read that after Christ's Ascension to the throne of God:

> Now war arose in heaven, Michael and his angels fighting against the dragon; and the dragon and his angels fought, but they were defeated and there was no longer any place for them in heaven. And the great dragon was thrown down, that ancient serpent, who is called the Devil and Satan, the deceiver of the whole world—he was thrown down to the earth, and his angels were thrown down with him. And I heard a loud voice in heaven, saying, "Now the salvation and the power and the kingdom of our God and the authority of his Christ have come, for the accuser of our brethren has been thrown down, who

accuses them day and night before our God. And they have conquered him by the blood of the Lamb and by the word of their testimony, for they loved not their lives even unto death. Rejoice then, O heaven and you that dwell therein! But woe to you, O earth and sea, for the devil has come down to you in great wrath, because he knows that his time is short!"

Note: After the Ascension of Christ, Satan was denied access to heaven and thrown down to the earth. He came down in great wrath, knowing that he had only a short time before his final end. His "great wrath" is manifested in the persecution of the Church, as the rest of the Book of Revelation makes clear.

This means that the persecution Christians may be called upon to endure in this age is part of a larger picture, a battle in a larger and longer war—a war that began when Satan was cast out and fell to the earth enraged. The angels fight along with us, as do the saints in heaven through their prayers. This does not make the pain hurt any less, but it at least gives cosmic meaning to what happens in our little lives.

Or perhaps the pain *may* hurt a little less? In the story of *The Martyrdom of Perpetua and Felicity* (5:2), we learn that Felicity was eight months pregnant when she was arrested. She was imprisoned with other Christians who were to be executed by being thrown to wild beasts. Felicity had a difficult delivery, and during the labor, one of the jailors asked her, "You who are in such suffering now, what will you do when you are thrown to the beasts?" She responded, "Now it is I that suffer what I suffer, but then there will be another in me, who will suffer for me, because I am about to suffer for Him."[13] In other words, the pain of martyrdom brings with it the grace of the Holy Spirit and the strength to endure that comes from Him.

It is all up to the Lord. But ultimately the suffering of martyrdom is a door—a doorway into eternal glory. All true Christians will find rest

---

13   "The Passion of the Holy Martyrs Perpetua and Felicity," *New Advent*, accessed September 30, 2025, https://www.newadvent.org/fathers/0324.htm.

for their souls as they pass from this life into the next. The martyrs find more than rest; they find reward, a reward beyond all imagining, a reward that undoes and confounds all the earthly mathematics of suffering. Saint Paul found it. Perpetua and Felicity found it. Martyrs of the twenty-first century are finding it even today.

Dateline Today

To Live Is to Suffer

IN WOODY ALLEN'S PARODY *Love and Death*, the character Sonja responded to the widow Natasha's tale of woe by saying, "To love is to suffer." We have suggested that this should be revised to say, "To *live* is to suffer," for suffering is woven into the fabric of existence. The suffering varies in intensity, duration, and complexity. One can know suffering from betrayal, from bereavement, from poverty, sickness, or persecution—from what Shakespeare calls "the thousand natural shocks that flesh is heir to."[14] Suffering seems to be unfairly and unevenly distributed, a reality that

---

14   *Hamlet*, Act 3, Scene 1.

adds to the suffering we must endure. Good people suffer, while bad people seem not to suffer—at least not to suffer as they deserve. What is the answer? How should we deal with suffering?

We sometimes see people whose heroism in the face of suffering inspires us. One such person was Jane Kristen Marczewski, better known by her stage name "Nightbirde." Jane was from Ohio, born on December 29, 1990. When she was diagnosed with breast cancer in 2017, her husband asked to divorce her. In 2018, she was declared cancer free. Cancer returned in 2019, and she was again declared cancer free in 2020. The cancer returned yet again, metastasizing into her lungs, liver, and spine.

In 2021, she auditioned as a contestant on the television show *America's Got Talent*, singing her own composition, "It's Okay." She sang about her life and insisted that it was all "okay." In explaining the song to her *America's Got Talent* judges, she said, "You can't wait until life isn't hard anymore before you decide to be happy. I'm so much more than the bad things that happen to me."[15] Although

---

15   *America's Got Talent Wiki*, https://agt.fandom.com/wiki/Nightbirde#Audition.

she received the judges' highest accolade and a "golden buzzer," Nightbirde had to withdraw from the competition before the quarterfinals because her cancer progressed. She died on February 19, 2022. She was just thirty-one years old.

Her approach is, of course, one way to handle suffering, and there is much wisdom to emulate in the life of this dear and heroic young woman. Like Nightbirde, we can make a decision to embrace whatever happiness the moment has for us, bravely saying to the world: "It's okay. You don't need to feel sorry for me. I am living in the moment and appreciating whatever good I can find there."

But Christians look not only to earthly heroes and heroines but also to our heavenly Lord and His Church. He is the final answer—not just to suffering but to everything. And our search for answers must include the Bible, beginning with the Bible's book about suffering, the Book of Lamentations, which we have been studying. What are the lessons of that book? Or, since it does not offer us a set of lessons like a Sunday School curriculum but rather a series of prayers in the dark, perhaps we should ask, "What do we find there?"

We find several things. First of all, we find a courageous and thorough acknowledgment of the magnitude of suffering, with no attempt to minimize it, dismiss its significance, deny its existence, or hide from it. Catastrophe is faced head-on in all its devastating power, whatever damage this may wreak on our tidy theology or worldview. Because we Christians believe that God is good and just, we are sometimes tempted to save God's reputation by minimizing the horrific effects of the suffering He sends or allows. We want to keep God out of the dock, as it were, by denying the moral significance of the disasters He allows. It is a temptation the Book of Lamentations will not permit us to make. Suffering is suffering, and it must be squarely faced, however inconvenient it may be to our cheerful theodicies.

Secondly, Lamentations reminds us that we are sinners, people with minds so blinded and hearts so dulled that we are in no position to judge or pass sentence on God. In every chapter of this book, we find this acknowledgment of sin as the authors

realize and confess that the disaster that overtook Jerusalem and Judah was their own fault, the
result of their sin.[16] Saint Paul would later remind
us that in this age "we see in a mirror dimly," that
our knowledge is partial (1 Cor. 13:12). How much
more then the self-knowledge of our own sins?
It may seem to us that we suffer more than we
deserve. The Book of Lamentations suggests that it
is not so. "Should any man living complain about
the punishment of his sins?" (3:39). Hardly!

Thirdly, Lamentations bids us to trust that our
suffering somehow forms part of a future eternal
and cosmic program of justice. In this age, injustice prevails as innocent people suffer oppression
from the powerful, who seem to evade justice
throughout their lives. This book assures us that it
will not always be so. Smug Edom's day will come
(4:22); indeed, a day will come to bring avenging
justice to *all* oppressors (3:64–66). It is too early,
therefore, to draw conclusions about God's justice.
He has not finished yet.

---

16   See 1:5, 1:14, 2:14, 3:39, 3:42, 4:6, and 5:16 for an impres-
      sive list.

Fourthly and finally, the Book of Lamentations invites us to trust God, no matter what our experience. We see this clearly in 3:21–33, in the very heart of the book, part of which reads:

But this I call to mind and therefore I have hope: / the steadfast love of Yahweh never ceases; / his mercies never come to an end; / they are new every morning. / Great is your faithfulness! / "Yahweh is all that I have," says my soul; / "therefore I will hope in Him." / Yahweh is good / to those who wait for Him, to the soul who seeks Him.

The book invites us to make trust in God central to our existence and to sit lightly on everything else, including our experience and the evidence of our senses. The trust it commends is therefore naked trust. It is not, however, blind trust, for it is based on our past experience of God's steadfast love. We allow past experience to judge present experience, giving more weight to His faithfulness and mercies than to our present suffering. The choice is ours.

Yet, as Christians, we confess that the full answer to anything cannot be found in the Old Testament Scriptures but only in Christ. That is because the Old Testament Scriptures were rooted in and bounded by the limitations of this age and this life. The full revelation and significance of the afterlife and of the age to come had not yet been revealed but only faintly foreshadowed, distantly adumbrated, with only the barest of hints and out-lines given.

For the Old Testament writers, this life was all there is; existence after death had no importance. The land of the dead, Sheol, was a land of shad-ows, a place where all the dead dwelt together, whether they were good or evil, a land of half-life and forgetfulness (Ps. 6:5 and 88:12). It was not a place where the just fared better than the unjust or where divine justice was meted out (see Is. 14:9; Eccl. 2:14–15, 3:19–22). That revelation about the afterlife would wait until the intertestamen-tal period and later (see, for example, the Book of Enoch and Luke 16:19f).

Given that, the Old Testament writers all located God's justice in this life and this age, declaring that His justice for us must somehow be manifested before we die. We see this over and over again in the Psalter, which threatens destruction for the wicked in this life—even though our experience tells us that it is not so. Those biblical declarations were not wrong. Justice *will* come, and the wicked *will* suffer what they deserve. But not always in this life. The New Testament reveals that much of God's justice is reserved for the afterlife and the age to come.

And that justice includes the reward and compensation given to those who suffer. It is not until we pass from this life that Christ will guide us to the springs of the water of life and wipe away every tear of suffering from our eyes (Rev. 7:17). It is not until then that we shall inherit the earth and know that our suffering in this age was preparing us for a burden of glory beyond all comparison (2 Cor. 4:17). By focusing exclusively on our suffering in this life and on the Old Testament texts, we miss one half of the entire moral equation. The Old Testament, reflecting the experiences of this life and age, can only pose the questions. The answers are not given until the New Testament, for the answers are all found in Christ.

Yet, we may still ask, Is the work of suffering confined to *this* age? Does suffering merely serve to pose the question and invite defiant trust? Is there no other purpose to suffering? I suggest that there is.

Suffering has been described as "God's megaphone" to get humanity's otherwise distracted attention.[17] Human beings have a fatal tendency and temptation to live without God and, especially in the affluent West, to live on the surface, superficially, absorbed in pleasures and entertainment, rarely reflecting, hardly giving a thought to deeper things. Suffering serves to crack us open, to make us ask questions we otherwise never would, to deepen our existence—to start us on the path to God.

It doesn't do this automatically or universally, of course. Some choose to respond to suffering by turning against God. Thus Proverbs 19:3 observes,

---

17   The phrase comes from a foreign title of C. S. Lewis's book *The Problem of Pain*.

"When a man's folly brings his way to ruin, / his heart rages against the LORD." But the way we respond to suffering remains a choice. We can choose not to harden our hearts but to let the suffering soften us and turn us back to God. Yet correlation is not causation, and it is perilous to insist that God allows suffering to bring us back to Him. For then why do those who have already turned back to God also suffer?

The truth is that there is an irreducible element of mystery to suffering since there is an equally irreducible element of mystery to life. It is, nonetheless, fair to observe that suffering does serve some purpose in the world, even if we cannot accurately trace all the ways and God's wisdom in all His dealings with humankind.

No discussion of suffering in the Christian life would be complete without reference to the Cross, the earliest and the universal symbol of the Christian Faith. It was through Christ's suffering of the Cross that the universe was washed clean from sin and reconciled to God; it was through the Cross that Christ's glory was revealed. Indeed, the Cross was not just a *prelude* to His Resurrection and ascended glory; it was *itself* His glory. It was His "hour" (John 12:27–28), the time when His glory was truly manifested to the world.

This means that suffering is now a path to glory, for Christ filled His suffering with His glory. He did not come to save us from suffering but rather to make suffering a means of communion with Him and a way to participate in His glory. When we suffer, He joins us in our suffering—not to *rescue* us from it but to *share* it. And in that sharing we are saved and transfigured, healed and glorified.

We see this most clearly in the suffering of martyrdom. When the martyr Felicity was about to suffer horribly by being mauled and eaten by wild beasts, she said that when she suffered in the arena, Another would suffer in her because she was about to suffer for Him. Note that Christ would suffer *in* and *with* her. He would not be present as an outside witness, an interested observer, but He would be there *in* and *with* her, making her suffering His own.

That is what St. Paul meant when he wrote to the Colossians that by his suffering for Christ, he was thereby completing what was lacking in His afflictions (Col. 1:24). Paul did not at all mean that there was something lacking or incomplete in Christ's suffering on the Cross. Rather, he was speaking of Christ's suffering *in His Body the Church*. In the suffering of Christians, Christ also suffers. The Church's suffering in this age is part of God's preordained plan, and Paul by his suffering was contributing to the fulfillment that plan.[18]

The point is this: We do not suffer alone. When God sends or allows suffering, He remains with His people, suffering along with them and in them. When we find Christ in our suffering, our suffering—and we with it—is transfigured.

Living without suffering is not possible, for God has indeed woven suffering into the very fabric of life. But suffering does not have to crush us. It can unite us more deeply and lastingly to the Lord. We can even confess with calm hearts that for us "to live is to suffer" because, as St. Paul once said, for us to live is Christ.

---

18   That is also what Paul meant when he wrote in Romans 8:17 that we co-suffer (συμπάσχω/sum*pascho*) with Christ, sharing His suffering on the Cross through our own little crosses. It is also what he meant in Philippians 3:10 about "sharing His sufferings."

Father Lawrence Farley was born in Toronto and was converted to Christ in the early 1970s. He was ordained a priest in the Anglican Church in 1979 and was received into the Orthodox Church in 1985. He attended St. Tikhon's Seminary for two years and was ordained to the Orthodox priesthood in 1986, returning to Canada to found an Orthodox mission in British Columbia in 1987. At the end of 2024 Fr. Lawrence retired as the founder and rector of the parish. He continues to write and lives in Surrey, B.C., with his wife, Donna. They have two children and six grandchildren.

We hope you have enjoyed and benefited from this book. Your financial support makes it possible to continue our nonprofit ministry both in print and online. Because the proceeds from our book sales only partially cover the costs of operating **Ancient Faith Publishing** and **Ancient Faith Radio**, we greatly appreciate the generosity of our readers and listeners. Donations are tax deductible and can be made at **www.ancientfaith.com.**

To view our other publications,
please visit our website:
store.ancientfaith.com

ANCIENT FAITH
R A D I O

Bringing you Orthodox Christian music,
readings, prayers, teaching, and podcasts
24 hours a day since 2004 at
www.ancientfaith.com